The
Success
Zone

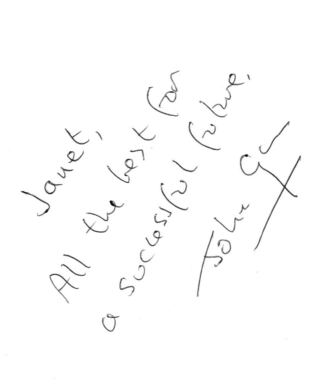

Janet,
All the best for
a successful future.

John G

The
Success
Zone

5 Powerful Steps to
Growing Yourself and Leading Others

Andrew Mowat   John Corrigan   Doug Long
Australia's innovative leadership experts

First Edition 2009

Copyright © 2009 by Author Name Here.

National Library of Australia
Cataloguing-in-Publication entry:

Author Name, Year
Book Title
Book Subtitle

1st ed.
ISBN: 9781921630040 (pbk.)

1.
2

Dewey No.

Published by Global Publishing Group
PO Box 517 Mt Evelyn, Victoria 3140 Australia
Email.info@TheGlobalPublishingGroup.com

For Further information about orders:
Phone: +61 3 97361156 or Fax +61 3 86486871

Dedicated to the generous, caring, collaborative and optimistic: may we learn from your leadership towards creating a better world.

Andrew Mowat

Table of Contents

Acknowledgements

Our journey into the realms of our own Blue Zones has been rich and rewarding, as much for the people we have met, who have helped us and influenced our thinking as what we have found.

Our wives, **Jackie**, **Amparo** and **Angela**, all of whom have given us so much support in our Quest.

Our **children**, each and all of whom give us the inspiration to create a better (Bluer) world for them.

Doreen Wilson, Principal, Balmain High School where this all started!

Our first group of schools in Victoria: Swan Hill SC, Montmorency SC, Narre Warren P-12, Pakenham SC, Wanganui Park SC, Brunswick SC, Kurranjang SC.

Matt Church, who has generously helped us apply the blowtorch of clarity.

Juan Aguilera, who inspired us with his work around conversations, thus assisting us to understand how this maps into the brain, and the growth of both organisations and individuals.

Helen and **Iain Crossing** who stimulated us to expand our work into the more general case of adults in work settings.

John Doherty and **Ron Lake** from The Department of Education and Early Childhood Development (DEECD) in Victoria, Australia some of our earliest supporters and mentors; and **Morris Sleep**, former principal of Wanganui Park SC in Shepparton who has supported us throughout.

Acknowledgements

Ron Lake, **Rob Blachford** (now in the UAE) and **Wayne Craig**, along with the staff of the Loddon Mallee, Western Metropolitan and Northern Metropolitan regions of The Department of Education and Early Childhood Development (DEECD) in Victoria, Australia, all of whom have supported us significantly.

The Durham Leadership Center and Durham County Council's Children and Young People's Services for their unending support and willingness to trust our knowledge and process. The following people have been significant for their contribution to our growth: **Dave Ford, Gerard Moran, Phil Hodgson, Kim Easton, Alison Young, Carole Payne, Carole Stansfield, Madeleine Walton, Sarah Brandon, Fay Murray, Liam Cairns, Ron Rooney; Steve Harness** and **Christine Forsyth** from Woodham CTC; **Sue Byrne** and **Kath Bennett** from Sunnydale Community College and many others from schools we have worked with in Durham).

The City of York Council's Learning, Culture and Children's Services particularly **Jill Hodges, John Catron** (now at Middlesbrough Council's Children, Families & Learning Department) and **Tim Holmes** and **John Tomsett**, and **Ian Price** from Huntington School.

Helen Jenner at **Tower Hamlets Children's Services** who has been unfailingly supportive of our work.

Bill Watkin at Specialist Schools and Academies Trust (SSAT) for his kind support and encouragement throughout.

Matthew Smerdon at Barings Foundation, Community Links and the Council On Social Action (COSA), one of the most blue zone people we

Acknowledgements

know who has been unfailingly supportive and helpful from the first moment he met John.

Anne Isaacs and **Zoe Blake** of Executive Action deserve mention, Anne because she has been instrumental in starting John on this journey and Zoe because she is helping us to get to a larger audience.

Jonah Lehrer, whose expert writings and commentary on the impact of neuroscience on our real world has helped shape our understanding of the brain.

Marion Janner, who so generously allowed us to share her story of borderline personality disorder as a way of illustrating Red and Blue Zones.

Kerrie & **Lyndon Phipps** for their generosity in starting the publishing journey for us, and for their collegiality, support and friendship.

Norm Dean for his quiet but constant unconditional belief in our journey a true Blue Zone champion.

Scott R McGrew, Annette Holland, Phyllis Rogers for their twitter friendship and early manuscript assistance.

Darren Stephens, Daryl and **Andrew Grant**, and **Jo Munro**, for their leadership, mentorship and assistance in bringing this book to life.

Catholic Education Office in **Melbourne Diocese** who have been very supportive of us over time particularly **Rosalie Jones, Adrian McGee, Mary Tobin** and **Helen Thomas**.

Catholic Education Office in **Sandhurst Diocese** who have been unfailing in their support particularly **Jim Rolfe, Audrey Brown, Bern**

Acknowledgements

Florence and **Pauline Fisher**.

Peter Stephenson for helping us to get our coaching program started.

Jerry Connor and **Sue Stokely** of Coach in a Box who helped us to structure our programs more systematically.

Chris Ryan, NSW Department of Education.

Anne Timothy and **Bernie Thomson** for helping us to get connected and get real in England.

Maree McKeown and **Richard Gersh** for their friendship, collegiality and leadership - two of the three musketeers!

Results Coaching Systems for helping Andrew on his 'coaching way'.

We would like to acknowledge all **the schools we have worked** with. It has been through struggling to understand how we create the ideal conditions for our children to grow that we have developed the understanding reflected in this book. A full list of the schools (at the time of writing)   1 in New South Wales, 110 in Victoria and 21 in England: Balmain High School, Wanganui Park SC, Narre Warren P-12, Brunswick SC, Kurunjang SC, Montmorency SC, Pakenham SC, Swan Hill SC, Bacchus Marsh SC, Glenroy KODE School, Mildura KODE School, Morwell KODE School, Swan Hill KODE school, Fitzroy HS, Boort PS, Boort SC, Camp Hill PS, Eaglehawk North PS, Eaglehawk SC, Flora Hill SC, Golden Square SC, Kangaroo Flat SC, Kennington PS, Maple Street PS, Mildura Special School, Pyramid Hill College, Red Cliffs East PS, Echuca College, Weerona College, Gisborne PS, Kyneton SC, Kyneton PS, Mildura PS, Maryborough, Preston West Primary School, Ivanhoe East PS, Lalor Secondary College, Roxburgh College, Ascot Vale West

Acknowledgements

Primary School, Brimbank College, Iramoo Primary School, Keilor Downs College, Monmia Primary School, Sydenham-Hillside PS, St Paul's, Queen of Peace, Mount St Joseph's Altona, St Mary's, St Francis of Assisi, St Monica's Epping, Emmaus College, St Luke's, St Scholastica's Bennettswood, St Benedict's Burwood, Nazareth College, St Elizabeth's, St Justin's, St Gerard's, Loyola College, St Damian's, St Martin of Tours, St Mary's, Thomas Carr College, CRC St Albans, Holy Eucharist, Sacred Heart, St Paul's School, Our Lady of the Sacred Heart, St Andrew's, St James's College, St Peter's, Bethany Catholic School, St James the Apostle, St Peter Apostle, St Joseph's Ferntree Gully, Marcellin College, Samaritan College, Parade College Bundoora, CBC St Kilda, St Joseoph's North Melbourne, Siena College, Aquinas College, CRC North Keilor, St Mary's Primary School - Myrtleford, St Joseph's Primary School - Chiltern, St Mary's Primary School - Rutherglen, Frayne College - Baraduda, Sacred Heart Primary School - Yarrawonga, St Augustine's Primary School - Wodonga, St Monica's Primary School - Wodonga, St Michael's Primary School - Talangatta, St Joseph's Primary School - Benalla, Myrtleford - Marian College, Sacred Heart PS Corryong - Corryong, St John's Euroa PS - Euroa, St Joseph's Primary School - Beechworth, St Augustine's College, St Mary's of the Angels SC, Notre Dame College, Catholic College Wodonga, St Joseph's Primary School, St Francis' Primary School, St Josephs Primary School, St Patrick's Primary School, St Mary's Primary School, St Joseph's Primary School, St Mary's Primary School, St Brendan's Primary School, St Luke's Primary School, St Mel's Primary School, Sacred Heart Primary School, Harris Academy South Norwood, Lambeth Academy, Bristol Brunel Academy, St Michael and All Angels CofE Academy, Academy 360, Duchess's Community High School, Highdown School and Sixth Form

Acknowledgements

Centre, Harbinger Primary School, Holy Family RC Primary School, Redlands Primary School, Bangabandhu Primary School, Greencroft Comprehensive School, Mayhill Junior School, Huntington School, Hermitage School, Sunnydale Community College, Woodham CTC, St John's RC College, Tudhoe Grange, Sedgefield, St Bede's.

Chapter 1

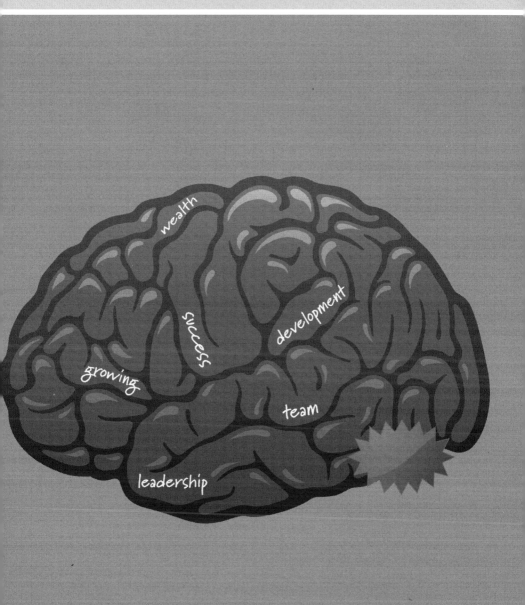

Introduction

Ah! my poor brain is racked and crazed,

My spirit and senses amazed!

Johann Wolfgang Von Goethe (from Faust, 1808)

Cancer. Illness. Business failure. Relationship failure. Redundancy. The three of us have experienced many of life's great challenges. Together we run three organisations: *Group 8 Management, Group 8 Education* and *emergent•blue.* Our vision? To create a world without fear, where anxiety is not a driving influence, where people can use the best of their brains.

Matt Church, Sydney-based entrepreneur, public speaker and author would say that leadership is all about turning fear into confidence, creating clarity from confusion and mobilising people in the pursuit of a better future. This, then, would be a fitting description for our work, and this book.

"...leadership is all about turning fear into confidence, creating clarity from confusion and mobilising people in pursuit of a better future." Matt Church

We, John, Doug and Andrew, as authors, have been shaped by our diverse journeys:

Doug's Introduction:

I was 57 when it happened to me.

I had forgotten a truth I had heard many years before: "The very things that made you successful in the past are what will probably cause you to fail in the future".

I couldn't believe it. Denial caused me to make more bad decisions and the situation worsened. I became angry. Very angry. The people with whom I spoke sought to apportion blame. Many of those I had considered friends seemed now to be unavailable when I phoned or emailed.

On the surface I was calm and positive. Underneath I was seething – mainly at myself and my own stupidity. I ceased to trust other people.

A year passed. I met a person who showed me a different manner. He saw beyond my anger, guilt and cynicism to the person underneath. He accepted me unconditionally. Inadvertently I opened up a little. Without being asked, he opened a door and I was invited to speak at a major conference in Japan – it even paid a good fee as well as all expenses.

It was as though I had been reborn. Rebuilding could now commence.

Andrew' s Introduction:

I still remember the anxiety, as a nine year old, of whether I would wake up in the morning or not. For a small period of time, falling asleep was plagued by a fear of not waking, of dying without me knowing. My prefrontal cortex had developed to the point of both feeling amazed that 'this is me, really me' and that 'this me' will end one day. In so doing, my brain replicated a process that we all go through, consciously or not, a process that seems unique to the human condition. The realisation of our identity and the some-day end of our identity begins the tug-of-war in the brain between the prefrontal cortex and the reptilian brain, between the architecture of knowing our future and of survival instinct.

This battle of 'minds' was to be repeated with far more energy and immediacy. The memory of the moment I was told I had cancer has never left me. Friday June 16 1995. If I immerse myself in the memory of the moment, the flood of anxiety and fear flowing from the pit of my stomach down though my legs is easily recalled. The double hit of "its melanoma and it has metastasised to your lymph system" that caused my world to stop more than momentarily remains within easy cognitive and emotional access. Yet, as a memory, it is one I rarely recall.

While this is not primarily about my recovery, a part of my approach to healing my cancer had a profound impact on both the restoration itself and on my life ever since. One tactic in dealing with my multitude of fears - fear of death, fear of not seeing my then two year old daughter grow up amongst others - was to develop a deep meditation technique triggered by evocative music. While this was by no means unique or earth shattering on its own, the twice-daily exposure to such meditation changed my brain. This change was long lasting and significant for the capacity it has given me since.

Interestingly, neither is this experience unique. Many cancer survivors have a living sense of having conquered, amongst many things, fear of death. For this 'victory' over fear, such people are often calm, flexible and highly adaptive in their post-cancer lives. Indeed, they often attribute this new capacity to the experience of cancer, and say that they are better for it.

John's Introduction:

My wife is Colombian, from one of the hottest parts of South America, and we moved to England after five years of marriage so that she could learn English (since leaving Colombia we had learned Italian together!). She hated the climate - amongst other things - from day one but our eldest daughter was 2 weeks old so she had a lot to do. We bought a house and I remember vividly the day we moved in thinking, is this it? Is this all there is? Over the next seven years we had two more children, consequently we kept ourselves busy. By 1995 I had the nagging feeling that I really had to find a place to live with a hot climate for Amparo and the sorts of professional opportunities that would interest and challenge me.

I was made redundant and my first thoughts were about finding another job - what with five mouths to feed and a mortgage to pay. I started the grind of looking. Completely by chance, I met three people in one week, all in London, who said "...why not go to Australia?" Even though I thought it would lead nowhere I felt a niggling need to follow this up. I emailed and called a raft of head hunters and consultants – no-one was particularly interested – but I managed to set up three appointments. I then thought I had better get a ticket and go although it seemed like a lot of money with little likely to show for it.

In Sydney I got on the phone and called everyone who had turned me down and I got a few more appointments. I ended up having 22 business meetings in the 5 working days I was there as I got referrals from the meetings that I had set up and, as I was only in town for a few days, people would squeeze me in. I flew home and two days later I received a job offer. We sold up and moved.

My mind – my brain – was guiding me in ways that I could not fathom then, leading me towards a way to meet my goals. Nothing rational, just feelings.

Each of the three of us, and indeed most who read this book, have explored the uncertain landscape of purpose and meaning. We have had the universe throw us together, with vastly different backgrounds, expertise and histories, yet with very similar questions. This book is a summary of the work begun by John back in 2001, and picked up by Doug, then Andrew as each of us joined the journey. It is a snapshot of our collective learning and wisdom, initially through a vision of an education system where everybody thrives. The journey has taught us much, but particularly that the learning and growth thrust upon us through our work has been both revolutionary (not evolutionary) and transferable. In the past, the common wisdom has been that the skills of engagement are a birth outcome, not a learning outcome. We have found that once a framework of understanding and a common language of engagement are in place, people have a point of reference from which they, themselves can grow.

This book, then, sets out a process of providing the necessary conditions for people to grow in a range of complex and diverse intelligences. It explores what people need from leaders, from teachers, from parents in order to be bright, collaborative and creative contributors to our world. It will show you how a 21st century brain is different from a 20th century brain, and why our planet is desperate for 'Blue Zone' brains. Further, by understanding this 'Success Zone' of your brain, this book will show you how to create prosperous outcomes for yourself, and for those around you.

Through each of the five steps, you will, yourself, mirror our journey into having greater life meaning and contribution.

These five steps include:
1. A language for the mind
2. Staying calm under pressure
3. Powerful questioning
4. Learning to listen
5. Conversations for growth

We often hear, of our work, that "it's not rocket science". Indeed it's not: in a world riddled with multiple layers of complexity it has become easy to lose touch with plain old common sense. A favourite quote explains this complexity:

"There is a theory which states that if ever anybody discovers exactly what the Universe is for and why it is here, it will instantly disappear and be replaced by something even more bizarre and inexplicable. There is another theory which states that this has already happened."
Douglas Adams

This book won't solve the 'mystery of the Universe', but it will solve one other: the enigma of engagement and influence, of great leaders, inspirational teachers and nurturing parents.

Chapter 2

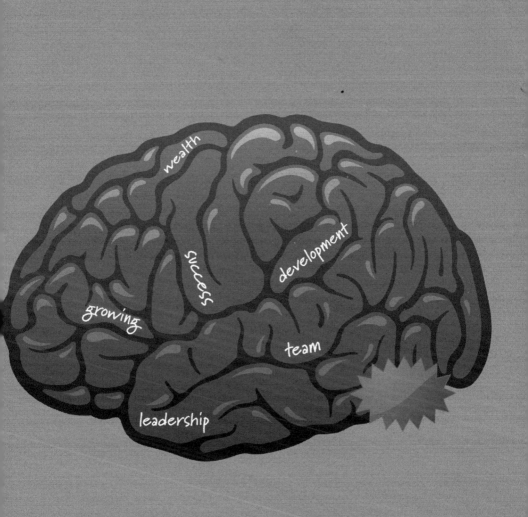

Three Brains, Two Minds

If your emotional abilities aren't in hand, if you don't have self-awareness, if you are not able to manage your distressing emotions, if you can't have empathy and have effective relationships, then no matter how smart you are, you are not going to get very far.
Daniel Goleman

Meeting Marion

We met Marion at a social change conference in London recently. A small, yet energetic woman who runs a highly successful national mental health project in the UK , she was accompanied by a little dog wearing a slightly askew, bright yellow 'support dog' jacket. When she was asked how her dog, Buddy, helps her was direct and open. "I have borderline personality disorder, and my self-harming puts me at very high personal risk. When I'm out with Buddy, I have to keep myself safe so that she is safe.".

Shortly after this somewhat unexpectedly upfront introduction, Marion became the first person, conversationally with us, to use the term 'amygdalae' when describing her emotional states. As people who regularly teach others about the amygdalae, two small components of our brain that alert us to threat, having such a spontaneous discussion about this part of the brain engaged his interest immediately.

Three Brains In One

We'll return to Marion shortly, but before we do, let's take a moment to construct a picture of the brain. We must be careful here: the brain is complex and interconnected beyond comprehension. It does not organise itself to fit our convenient models and metaphors. Increasingly, a geographical approach to categorising brain regions, while it serves us well at the macro level, is being shown by research to have its limits.

For some time now, a reasonably well agreed-upon model of the brain is the tripartite - a brain that consists of three broad regions or layers.

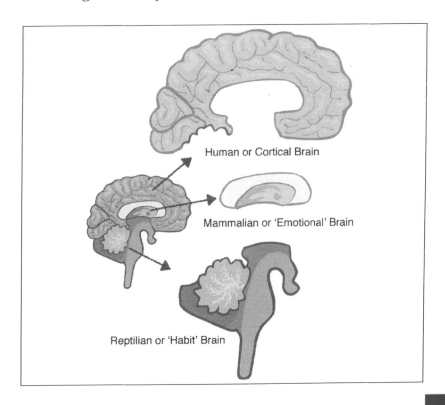

Human or Cortical Brain

Mammalian or 'Emotional' Brain

Reptilian or 'Habit' Brain

The deepest layer is the "**reptilian brain**", contained in the brain stem. This part of the brain is concerned with biological survival more than anything else. Found at the very base of the skull, where it meets your neck, this region manages automatic biological and vital control functions. Breathing, heart rate, blood electrolyte balance, swallowing and object tracking with the eyes and the startle response are a few of the functions controlled by this region. The jump you get from hearing a car backfire - the startle response - is also an outcome of the 'circuitry' here.

The mid-brain, sometimes referred to as the "**mammalian brain**" and at other times the "**limbic** system", is the centre of feeling and emotion. Seen largely as an evolutionary outcome resulting from the greater investment of parental care. It is, indeed, a section of the brain that is unique to mammals. Increasingly neuroscience is uncovering this region as one of the most significant in our day-to-day lives. Jonah Lehrer, in his recent book "How We Decide", has expertly crystallised the emerging view that the emotional brain is responsible for a great deal more, particularly in making decisions, than we ever could have imagined. A growing body of research suggests that the rational brain, the neocortex, lags behind, creating the cognitive justification for what has already happened in the emotional brain.

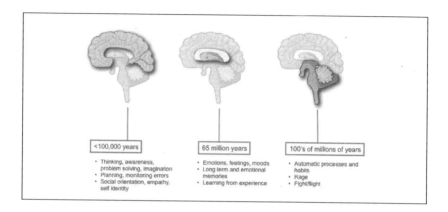

The most recent and most advanced layer is the outer **neocortex**, or 'new brain' which exists only in mammals and is highly developed in humans. We will also refer to this most evolutionary recent brain as the 'human' brain, since it is this region that gives us our humanity. Indeed, much of what differentiates us from other advanced forms of life has its home here. Language, imagining a different future, reasoning and knowing how someone else feels from their expression alone are but a few 'miracles' of the new brain. Even the beginnings of complex movements such as reaching to catch a ball after tracking its movement through the air seem to begin in the human brain.

One very special region of the neocortex is the **prefrontal** cortex, essentially found behind your forehead. In the first half of the twentieth century, this part of the brain was thought to have no significant role to play. So much so, that it was seen as an expendable casualty in personality modification through lobotomy. Modern neuroscience research tells a completely different story. Indeed, the myriad of functions that the neocortex plays a significant, or even partial role in, abound.

Let's just for a moment take an inventory of what research currently tells us that the prefrontal cortex influences or controls in some way:

- Reflection, daydreaming and mindfulness
- Consideration of options
- Imagination and creativity
- Considering the future, setting goals and tracking progress towards them
- Monitoring errors (social, cognitive and emotional)
- Understanding and labelling of the emotions of the self
- Understanding and knowing the emotional state of others
- Managing impulses
- Affiliation, generosity and goodwill
- Integration of emotional, rational and intuitive information into decision making
- Core personality
- Development of a moral framework and applying behaviour according to those morals

It may not surprise you to know that those who we could name as socially, occupationally and financially successful would also be people who have high functioning prefrontal cortices.

Thinking about the way that we experience the world, both internally and externally, provides a somewhat false sense that a singular mind is responsible. We remain significantly unaware of the operation and impact of any of the many 'sub-systems' in the brain responsible for this 'singular experience' of the world. Some of these systems are inaccessible and buried well below our consciousness, yet others remain tantalisingly within reach once we build awareness and target attention.

Further, some of these brain sub-systems seem to collaborate, while others work in opposition. "The McGurk effect" demonstrates the difference in outcomes when subsystems combine - try this experiment yourself by visiting **http://www.thesuccesszone.com/resources** to have a first hand experience in engaging systems below your consciousness. Note that the effect explored in this video is not under conscious control - the two subsystems explored here exert their collaboration beyond your control.

Decision-making In The Three Brains

The reptilian brain makes decisions efficiently, instinctively, habitually and impulsively. Decisions made in this region lack the learning from experience, or intuition, of the mammalian brain, and the rational and considered approach of the human brain. Survival situations remain the only purposeful and appropriate aspect of using this brain region for decision-making in today's world.

The mammalian brain is a surprisingly powerful decision-maker based on its ability to process a large number of variables in the light of its own experience. When we become expert in something and "know" what to do then it is this brain that is "speaking" (and being pre-verbal this appears as a feeling). Similarly, if we want to buy a house then the optimal decision-making process is to visit a range of houses and then buy the one that "feels" right. Intuition is another name for this ability to feel what the right thing to do is. When this is the prevailing decision-making process then organisations tend to grow hierarchically with the best decision-makers taking leading roles. The once all-powerful principal in a school reflected the dominant role of this brain type. This works very well in stable or slowly changing conditions.

When we have new problems to solve then the human brain is the place from which to operate. It is enormously powerful but inefficient. We can only hold about four variables in this brain at one time so that if we have a new, complex problem (say with 30 variables) then it needs a team of people to be able to solve it. This team needs to operate in human brain mode and in such an environment that all variables are properly aired, an environment of openness and acceptance. Under these conditions the mammalian brain can get to work to process the variables and after a time it will become obvious to the group what the solution is.

As you will see later in this book, the greater the presence and level of anxiety, the greater the tendency towards reptilian-brain decisions being made.

Your Two Mind States

One explicit goal of this book is to build your awareness, and your ability to express your awareness, around certain mind states that arise from the interaction of your brain's three 'subsystems'.

Consider the following situation:

You are in a nice restaurant waiting for your meal whilst having an engaging conversation with your partner around planning an exciting upcoming holiday. You begin to notice that first one table, then more are being served their meals, though you are sure that you ordered before them.

Your attention now gradually begins to drift away from your immersed planning to scanning and watching for more evidence. As your observations are confirmed, you unsuccessfully try to catch the eye of the waiter, who is clearly serving others who ordered well after you. Very soon, your ability to engage at a thinking level is reduced dramatically in proportion to the increase in the 'gut response'.

As this situation progresses, your whole experience is hijacked by an emotive response, characterised by feelings of anger, increased heart rate, raised voice, and strong eye contact and body language. You even notice that you are now not as hungry...

This is an example of a shift in brain resources *from* a mind state that we call the **Blue Zone** to a different mind state called the **Red Zone**. As this shift progresses, you find yourself thinking and connecting less as more 'primal' feelings occur. Indeed, your brain has detected a threat and is preparing you at many levels.

As such situations deteriorate, you literally get to the point where thinking and executive control - managing verbal, even physical impulses - becomes impossible. We will describe the "Blue Zone" and "Red Zone" states in detail shortly. Before we do, one important piece of framework needs to be explained - your brain's 'bandwidth' limits.

The Brain's Bandwidth Limits

For an organ that comprises something around 2% of your total body weight, your brain has an energy demand of about 20% of your energy budget. Interestingly, this 20% energy usage tends to be fixed: you brain uses much the same energy when you are reading this, sleeping, doing a crossword, working or watching a movie.

The implications for this are far-reaching, particularly when considering the interactions of our two mind states - the

Blue Zone and Red Zones. Imagine that these mind states are each represented by a bucket. You only have enough resources to fill one bucket, so at any one time you may have half in each, or all in one bucket or the other. For you to have your Blue Zone operating at full capacity, resources are provided by 'the bucket' that the Red Zone might have ordinarily been using. Similarly, if your Red Zone becomes active, it does so, at a resource level, at the expense of the Blue Zone.

> "Just as there is a limit to how much internet traffic you can download on any connection, your brain analogously has similar attentional limits."

This limit of biological 'capital', particularly oxygen and glucose, available to the brain underpins another phenomenon: the scarcity of attention. Think of it as available bandwidth if you like. Just as there is a limit to how much internet traffic you can download on any connection, your brain analogously has similar attentional limits. You have a clear limit to how much bandwidth you can 'spend' on any one task - try listening to two people speaking at once. You will be intuitively aware that you simply cannot. You may switch your attention between the two voice 'streams', but never can you simultaneously listen and fully comprehend both. This simple illustration manifests itself silently in much of our world, largely because we remain unaware of how we are using our attention 'bandwidth'.

Your awareness on how and on what you pay attention to becomes critical when you consider that your attention drives what you learn and habituate, how effective you are socially and your ability to engage others. Indeed, attention is the currency of engagement. Those who use their attention well are themselves highly engaging, interesting and influential. We will be explicitly addressing how you direct your attention in the "Powerful Questioning" and "Learning to Listen" Chapters.

Given the limits to our attention and the high competition for that attention by many things in our day-to-day life, the brain has a process whereby it cycles through high demand priorities. We call this attention priority, a mind process where the most pressing attentional needs rise to the top, much like the way blobs of lava rise and fall in a lava lamp. Once the demand decreases, that issue 'cools' and falls out of our attention awareness. If left to its own device, the mind will be cycling through a range of attention priorities depending on your habits, needs and desires.

There is a high-energy cost to holding things out of this natural cycle - like paying attention to a speaker for more than thirty minutes - and the attention priority cycle will sneak back in whenever it can. We notice, in presenting workshops for instance, that if the temperature of the room becomes uncomfortably cool, the need of being comfortable rises above attending to us in terms of attention.

The thing is, while you remain unaware of this, you are largely unable to harness the incredible power of this process. You are slave to your habits, needs and desires. We even have our rational brain keep this state in play for us with justifying statements like "I don't have the time to do this right now". In fact, if you have ever stopped to think about this statement, a common one when we are faced with things we'd rather not do, why is it that some people find the time to do the tough things, and others do not? We all have the same amount of time - it is just that some of us do not prioritise in the same way.

There are a number of deliberate and intentional 'tricks' that are used to construct a different attention priority than our habits, needs and wants would have. Tricks such as affirmations and goals, for instance, allow us to hold at the top, in spite of the habituated priorities, new priorities that without effort would fall back to the bottom of the pile. Do this once - say by writing down your goals for the year - and for a while your brain can hold this as an attention priority for a short time. Soon, however, the energy cost of holding these goals at the 'top of mind' allows other needs, wants and habits to resume the cycle.

Action Zone: Attention Priority

The best way that you can harness attention priority is to wire your preferred future into desires, needs and habits. Do this with intention by:

- Speaking to as many people as you can around your passion, goals and future
- Writing and reading your goals on a daily basis
- Affirming daily the future you wish to create
- Reading as much as you can in your niche or field, then writing and speaking from your learning and perspective
- Increasing the scope of absorption by being in the best mind state - the Blue Zone

Next time you catch yourself saying "I don't have the time to do that" reframe it into "it is not a priority for me right now" (because, simply, it is not). Check on your emotional energy when you reframe - things that should be a higher priority will let you know!

A Language For The Mind: Blue Zone, Red Zone

Typically, we are not particularly 'brain aware': we do not have easily accessible language that allows us to articulate our current 'mind state'. This is particularly the case when our amygdalae are highly active - all we see is the "red mist" and we are immersed in our limbic response. Further, we are not generally used to monitoring our thinking or feelings, or indeed, which element of our brains might be active. Research, particularly from Matthew Lieberman and the Department of Social Psychology at UCLA, is showing that we have a greater chance of moderating our negative mind states when we can label them.

Hence, we have two mind states that we describe in this book: the **Blue Zone** and the **Red Zone.** These states approximately overlap the tripartite brain in the following way:

The Red Zone

The Red Zone describes the mind states that emerge while engaging with the collaboration between the *reptilian* and *mammalian* brains, the two 'oldest' and most efficient regions of our brain. In other words, the locus of control of the actions, behaviour, thoughts or feelings of a person stems from either the mammalian or reptilian brains. The Red Zone is associated with the drive to survive and is not particularly self aware, nor self-managing.

Recalling Marion's story, it would not surprise you that the issues that she faces arise out of an overactive Red Zone. To describe the Red Zone in a single concept, we would use anxiety: where anxiety exists, or the potential for anxiety to easily present, the Red Zone is active. When the Red Zone is active, it does so at the expense of the Blue Zone.

While the full range of emotions are available in the Red Zone, emotions characterised by responses to threat, fear or loss are more accessible in this state. Moreover, absence of awareness and control of feelings in this state creates huge potential to cascade and perpetuate further feelings, thoughts, moods, behaviour and even self perception.

In their book "A General Theory of Love", Lewis, Amini and Lannon use the elegant metaphor of emotions being like musical notes made by a piano. As the hammer strikes a string, a resonance that we detect as musical pitch occurs. Such is the case with emotions; when the resonance is strong enough to detect we have a feeling. Characteristically, the Red Zone has the ability to replay these notes without, itself, being able to discriminate between the original and 'echo' notes. Hence, negative emotions and feelings persist with us, each memory of the original trigger causing another hammer strike.

For Marion, this re-resonating occurs to such a degree that it *cascades* into feelings that result in self harm and even attempts on her life. As it turns out, Marion has an overactive limbic system, to the point where her conscious world narrows to consider only strategies that fulfil the self harm 'tape'. Her amygdalae become so active that they override her more considered 'impulse-managing' Blue Zone brain. Many of us have experienced something of Marion's condition, though most often without the drive towards self harm. Think of the last time that you really 'lost it'. Perhaps it was slamming a door, yelling at the kids or lashing out an inanimate object. Daniel Goleman, famed author of "Emotional Intelligence" would name this an *amygdala hijack*. In this moment, you were likely unable to think clearly, perhaps found it difficult to manage impulses and were very narrowly focused on the issue of the moment. This is the world of the 'Red Zone'.

For others the impact of the Red Zone that Marion experiences is often less dramatic, but no less an influence on their life. Take this story from a principal about a high performing teacher with an easily activated Red Zone:

Malcolm is a teacher I once worked alongside. When he had compliance in his classroom, he was a highly engaging and very popular teacher. He used a variety of instructional practices to create learning opportunities for his students and, not surprisingly, he often had outstanding results from his students. As Malcolm's principal, I had, on one occasion, no choice but to place a student with Asperger's syndrome in his class. This student challenged the very core values that Malcolm held: "I am the teacher and you will respect me". The interaction between these two intransigent, but in their own right worthy, people was fiery and socially destructive.

The trigger of this student behaving in a manner that challenged Malcolm's professional mores created a Red Zone 'cycling' cascade of
    "This student is not doing what I asked"
    "I am angry"
    "I am the teacher"
    "He should do as he is told"
    "I need to act and show authority"

While the conditions were predictable and understood, Malcolm was an outstanding teacher. When his environment changed, so too did his levels of anxiety. For Malcolm, the absence of awareness through being in the Red Zone put possible solutions and choices out of reach. Just as a baby's whole world is hunger when they are hungry, and just as Marion's whole world was pain when she was in her Red Zone, Malcolm became the very expression of his Red Zone. It was visible for all to see (and as we will see later, available for others to experience), leading eventually to his premature exit from an otherwise successful teaching career.

> "Indeed, as you will see from this point on, this Blue Zone mind state *is* the Success Zone."

The Blue Zone

The Blue Zone, clearly a very different mind state, is the overlap between the emotional mammalian brain and the neocortex, the 'human' brain, and particularly where the locus of *control* is in the human brain. Indeed, as you will see from this point on, this Blue Zone mind state is the Success Zone.

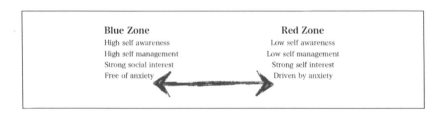

Blue Zone	Red Zone
High self awareness	Low self awareness
High self management	Low self management
Strong social interest	Strong self interest
Free of anxiety	Driven by anxiety

As was the case in the Red Zone, the full range of emotions are available to the Blue Zone, but critically the massive capacity of the prefrontal cortex, and all of its attributes shown above, is enlisted. This provides awareness and choice through the ability to think about emotions and thinking itself.

Take a 'good news' story chronicled by the "Daily Collegian" of Tampa in 2005:

Good news from Tampa – common decency may not be dead.

A few days ago, amid sweltering heat, a homeless mother living at a Salvation Army shelter with her five kids discovered a purse heavy with $800 in cash and two paychecks in a parking lot. Then she did the unthinkable – she returned it.

According to Tampa news sources, 24-year-old Canesha Blackman didn't even open the bag. She was quoted as saying that she would feel terrible if she lost money, and didn't want to put someone else through that trauma.

Imagine the full range of emotions and thoughts that this homeless mother might have gone through: joy at the find, uncertainty, empathy through imagining how the loser of the bag felt, the comparison against a moral framework, the decision to return the bag and the likely good feeling resulting from the generosity and honesty of the bag's return. While it is hard to know how aware she may have been, it is clear that she exercised strong choice in the matter, a element largely absent in the Red Zone.

The 'human' or cortical brain is complex beyond comprehension. However, even a cursory acknowledgement of its 'skill set' illuminates why a marriage between mammalian and cortical brains is so powerful. This cortical brain, amongst many things, provides:

- The ability to solve new problems
- An ability to plan, set goals and monitor errors
- A sense of who we are as individuals - self identity
- Imagination
- Empathy - knowledge and insight into the emotions of others

Essentially, the Blue Zone is characterized by social orientation, self-awareness, and through this awareness, an ability to choose or self-manage.

In our most recent meeting with Marion, she mentioned that her last 'event' was marked by a subtle but significant shift. In the middle of her limbic dominance and on the way to the toilet to self harm, she had the thought "I am in my red zone...". This was enough of a toe in the door for her to redirect the outcome and avoid yet another self-harming session. It was the emergence of Blue Zone awareness and choice. While her mood and feelings were still Red Zone, the impact of a fraction of the Blue Zone illustrates its huge potential for change and growth.

Conclusion

The Blue and Red Zones, then, are two mind states that are useful to identify and build awareness around. Note that this is all they are: Blue is not good and Red is not evil, they are just two different mind states. Hence, if you are in a Red Zone moment, you are not a bad person, you are just having a Red Zone moment. Each state has its use, its own ideal context. If you were to step off a curb into the path of a bus, you would find yourself back on the curb, heart beating, before your cognitive brain has a chance to think anything. The impulsiveness and speed of the Red Zone, here, is in its element: survival.

Using the Blue Zone to rescue you from the path of an oncoming bus is as ludicrous as its success short term. A Blue Zone response would be reflective, observational and considerate of options. Slow and cumbersome compared with the Red Zone, by the time you have considered the question "...if things could be perfect, how might they look now?" the bus has moved on, as have you.

Using the Red Zone to solve social issues is just as ridiculous. A system that prepares you only for a physical response in such an impulsive and unaware fashion cannot have much chance of success. Yet we continue to employ it in resolving conflict, managing people and coercing change. The rest of this book is about applying the Blue Zone to yourself, to helping others grow, to creating thriving organisations. Blue Zone principles will help you become a better communicator, a more influential leader and a more interesting person to be around.

> "Using the Red Zone to solve social issues is just as ridiculous. A system that prepares you only for a physical response in such an impulsive and unaware fashion cannot have much chance of success."

Action Zone: Red Zone Activation Exercise

Take a moment to think of situations that trigger a Red Zone response that is at least moderate in you. Use this exercise to build your awareness of aspects of your habituated Red Zone responses.

Where are you when this happens?
Who or what might have triggered the response?
How often do you experience a moderate to strong red zone response?
How quickly does it appear?
How quickly does it subside?
What are your dominant triggers? (Uncertainty, Lack of Control, Rejection, Unfairness, not being Listened to?)

Come back to this exercise after working with the methods for managing down your Red Zone. Check to see how you are progressing in shrinking your amygdalae!

Chapter 3

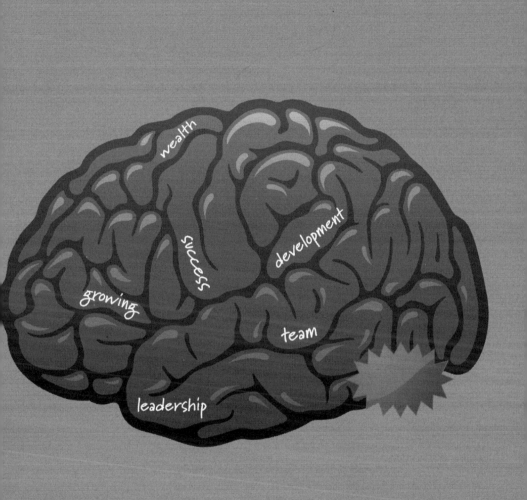

Your Mind Zones In Action

Comfort in expressing your emotions will allow you to share the best of yourself with others, but not being able to control your emotions will reveal your worst.

Bryant H. McGill

Imagine you are running to catch a train about to depart. You run to the platform that your train usually leaves from and you get on before you look to see (if at all) where it is going. This is a metaphor for the Red Zone. You are 'inside' the emotion, fully engaged and even consumed by it perhaps.

Now picture standing on an overpass to all platforms. You are watching trains arrive and depart from the platforms, perhaps knowing already the destinations of some or all of the trains. Knowing this, you choose to 'engage' with one of the trains as you please. This is the Blue Zone metaphor: knowing the destination, and perhaps even from where the trains have come, is the attribute of mindfulness or awareness that enables the next step: choice.

In either zone, the full range of emotions are present and available, and you may still fully engage with that emotion. There are people we know, as would you, that live most of their life in the Red Zone, yet are often happy people. In spite of this, the Red Zone very much limits the future development of such people. Only in the Blue Zone does awareness and choice open the door to significant growth.

The Celebrated Case Of Phineas Gage

Phineas Gage is now somewhat of a celebrity in books such as this. His story, in many ways, exposed potential secrets of the prefrontal cortex, one of the central players in the Blue Zone. On September 13, 1848, twenty-five-year-old Gage was working as a railroad construction foreman, blasting rock for the Rutland & Burlington Railroad Company near Cavendish, Vermont in the United States. After drilling a hole and adding sand and gun powder, his regular activity was to tamp down the mix using a large iron rod. On this occasion, the tamping process ignited the gunpowder mix, firing the iron rod as a projectile through his forehead. Amazingly he survived the accident, though with substantial damage to one or both of his frontal lobes.

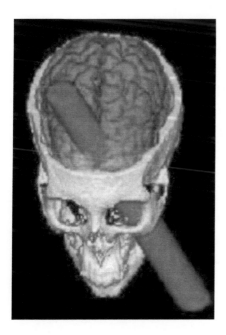

Effectively lobotomised, Phineas was conscious and physically well, beyond belief considering the scale of the injury. His treating doctor, John Martyn Harlow noted:

"You will excuse me for remarking here, that the picture presented was, to one unaccustomed to military surgery, truly terrific; but the patient bore

his sufferings with the most heroic firmness. He recognized me at once, and said he hoped he was not much hurt. He seemed to be perfectly conscious, but was getting exhausted from the hemorrhage. Pulse 60, and regular. His person, and the bed on which he was laid, were literally one gore of blood."

Indeed, he recovered to full physical health shortly after the accident, yet Harlow noted significant psychological consequences:

"...He is fitful, irreverent, indulging at times in the grossest profanity (which was not previously his custom), manifesting but little deference for his fellows, impatient of restraint or advice when it conflicts with his desires, at times pertinaciously obstinate, yet capricious and vacillating, devising many plans of future operations, which are no sooner arranged than they are abandoned in turn for others appearing more feasible."
John Martyn Harlow, (1848). "Passage of an iron rod through the head".

The outcomes from this case, and many others both accidental and deliberate since, have continued to confirm the critical nature of the prefrontal cortex as a participant, even leader, in the Blue Zone. While many areas, including those in the emotional brain, contribute to Blue Zone activity, it seems that the area behind your forehead is special indeed. Damage to this part of the brain can not only change your behaviour, but who you actually are.

Influential Leaders

Think for a moment on the one or two most positively influential teachers that you had as a student. Picture them, recall how it is you felt in their presence, what it was that they gave to you. When we ask people to do this, the most common answers are:

> They listened to me
> They respected me (in spite of how I might have behaved and/or performed)
> They challenged me
> They believed in me
> They were passionate about their subject, and what it could offer others

There may have been some other attributes, but generally, this list captures how most people answer. We have asked you to think of a past positively influential teacher here because this is often the most accessible example for people. This list also applies, however, to the most influential leaders or, indeed, to influential people generally.

We have also conducted extensive research with the students of today, and when we ask them "What makes a great school for you?", then we get the answers:

> A place where I am safe
> Where teachers listen to me
> Where teachers respect me
> Where teachers believe in me
> Where teachers know their subject, and know how to deliver it

These are in order, though the middle three might easily be interchanged with each other. When we ask students the follow-up question of "When these things are present for you, what happens?", the answers are just as clear:

I have more confidence to do the work and learn what I need to learn

I have (greater) respect for the teacher

I want to go out of my way not to let the teacher down.

Interestingly, the reference to confidence correlates to brain resources, particularly glucose and oxygen, being present where they are needed. Moreover, the more we test this against other contexts, such as leadership in general, the more we see that this seems to be emerging as a universal description of the elements and outcomes of effective engagement.

Think, then, of the most effective and inspirational leader that you have had in *recent* times. It is most likely that they themselves created professional safety for you, listened, respected and believed in you, and had the knowledge and skills of leadership. Through this, you most likely felt greater confidence in doing what you had to do, greater respect for the leader and a willingness to go out of your way for this individual or the organisation that they led. On this last point, where one leader out of many displays listening, respecting and believing, people tend to develop strong loyalty to this one leader, at the expense of other leaders. Where many or all leaders listen, respect and believe, people develop strong loyalty to the organisation.

Triggering Your Blue Zone

So what are the triggers that cause our brains to shift the balance to the Blue Zone? Resources are redirected when we detect:

- Generosity
- Vulnerability
- Inclusion
- Clarity and certainty
- Permission
- Acknowledgement
- Trust
- Safety (physical, professional, social and emotional)
- Being listened to
- Being believed in
- Being respected unconditionally
- Authentic and focused attention

Of the above list, where many of the elements overlap in some way, the last is the most significant. We would even go so far as to say that all of the triggers above the last are forms of authentic, focused attention. Indeed, deep engagement is triggered when a person detects that your attention on them is authentic, strong and *for them*. Where they detect that your attention, while perhaps remaining deep and real, is for *you*, the listener, engagement falls.

"Indeed, deep engagement is triggered when a person detects that your attention on them is authentic, strong and for them. "

You may have noticed already: attention is the common thread throughout this book. How you 'spend' your attention on yourself or others, and how aware you are of your use of attention, will largely determine your success, and the success of those you lead.

The Drive To Efficiency

There is a price to pay for using the Blue Zone: it is resource intensive. Studies have shown that you can be using up to five times as much energy in your Blue Zone, compared with brain regions associated with your Red Zone. So let's just take a step back, and look at some key points about your brain before we take a closer look at your Red Zone:

The most accessible part of your brain, for you, is the thinking brain - the neocortex. This is where you experience your thoughts, your senses, and through specialised parts of the neocortex, the emotional brain.

Most of your brain's activity is inaccessible to your conscious awareness. Some suggest, like an iceberg, that up to 90% of the activity in your brain is below the level of overt consciousness.

The more recent or 'modern' the 'equipment', the more energy it uses. Your brain stem, the reptilian brain, is the most efficient part of your brain in terms of energy consumption.

Given that your energy availability is a biological economy, and therefore limited at any moment in time, your brain will always take the path of efficiency if it can. Habits, which reside in your Red Zone, are always preferred over something new, which takes concentration, cognitive effort and resources.

The picture I am attempting to construct above is that a good part of your brain is not under your direct conscious control, and that it will 'decide' on a course of action, not from what might be' best', but what will be most efficient. This is why, when you have taken months to relearn a golf swing, under pressure you revert to your old habitual action. It is also why, perhaps after time spent repairing a relationship, under emotional pressure the dialogue reverts to the old argumentative scripts so easily.

All of this means that already your brain is biased towards choosing the path of the Red Zone over the Blue, if only because it wins the efficiency stakes.

Your Red Zone In Detail

The hallmarks of the Red Zone are immersion, lack of awareness and lack of strong and deliberate choice.

Oftentimes, the less intrusive and negative activities of the Red Zone just potter away in the background, so to speak. Remembering that the Red Zone is the mind state resulting from overlap between our limbic and reptilian brains, in any 'normal' moment, the Red Zone will not be intruding to any great degree. It is when we have a *mind state* that is strongly coloured and driven by the Red Zone, that it intrudes at the cost of the Blue Zone. While the most common and obvious forms of this intrusion are anger, guilt, anxiety and fear, the Red Zone also intrudes in a particularly impulsive way through blind love, lust and greed.

Our Red Zones are a vestige of a biological era where the imperative was physical survival. Amongst many things, our limbic system is alert for anything that might be *interpreted* as a physical threat, and responds both in the brain, and in the body. When activated, our threat-response system shuts down non-essential functions, like digestion, and blood flow is diverted from internal organs to muscles and extremities, in preparation for action: fight or flight. Take note of a really angry person and you will see this extra blood flow as flushing of the face. Eye pupils are dilated, heart and breathing rates are increased, the immune system is suppressed, and agents are released into the blood to assist in blood clotting. The body, then, is prepared for a *physical* response.

In terms of the impact of a perceived threat on thinking and emotions, this state brings a strong self-interested perspective, engages impulsive desires, resorts to pre-existing habits and expects the worst. The attention 'field' narrows, and tends to lock onto the cause of the threat. Creative thinking, which may well be needed for the resolution of the 'threat', is suppressed, as is the ability to read and understand the emotional state of others. Error tracking and monitoring, such as saying something inappropriate, is also suppressed.

This cachet of physiological and neurological reactions is all well and good, if you are indeed facing physical danger, but is far from helpful in the heat of an argument, managing a teenager or dealing with an angry customer. Moreover, the problem with Red Zone responses is that the amygdalae are so efficient at alerting us to threat, that without habituated awareness, they often have us reacting well before we have cognitive control. The preparation, mentally and somatically, for a physical resolution of the threat or stress is a poor strategy when we are actually called upon to settle the threat socially and/or emotionally. In the absence of physical resolution, no matter how well we have dealt with the situation, the biochemistry of the stressed state will persist longer.

The typical Red Zone response has been well exposed now, using fMRI brain scanning techniques. Far from theoretical conjecture, social cognitive neuroscience is illuminating such outcomes when subjects are exposed to stimuli such as rejection, ambiguity, perceived unfairness, not being listened to, and lack of perceived control. It is worth noting that in physical terms, none of these stimuli are life threatening. However, try telling your brain this: the physical, emotional and cognitive response driven by the activation of the Red Zone is as if our very lives were at stake. For people like Marion, where the Red Zone activation is dangerously *unbalanced*, lives can be at stake.

So let's look at the triggers that can get the Red Zone active:

- Fear, anxiety and guilt
- Rejection and exclusion
- Uncertainty and ambiguity
- Perceived unfairness
- Perceived lack of control
- Perceived or imagined loss
- Not being listened to
- Being judged
- Being told how to think, feel, or in some cases what to do.

Of all of the above, uncertainty, imagined or perceived loss and perceived lack of control are the most significant Red Zone triggers.

Emotional Contagion

Intuitively, we all know that emotions are contagious: how else do evocative stories have impact on us? Neuroscience seems to have uncovered the biomechanism for the catching of another's emotions: mirror neurons.

Mirror neurons are special nerve cells in the brain that fire both when someone performs an action, and when someone observes the same action performed by another person. These special cells are found in mammals, and even some birds. It seems that where there is some sort of social structure to a species, mirror neurons are present. These neurons, then, "mirror" the behaviour of another, as though the observer were themselves acting. In humans, brain activity consistent with mirror neurons has been found in the premotor cortex and the inferior parietal cortex, both significant regions of the 'modern' brain.

Empirical research suggests that these neurons allow us to understand the emotional state of others, and to adopt to some degree, those same emotions. Indeed, such research is showing that people with Autism spectrum disorders have reduced function, or reduced numbers of mirror neurons, suggesting an explanation to the social awkwardness for such people.

It seems that our ability to read, adopt and infer emotions is such a strong trait of our brains that we even attribute emotionality to inanimate objects. Test this out, if not on yourself, then on someone you know, by watching the Ikea Lamp advertisement (on our resources page – http://www. thesuccesszone.com/resources). Ask yourself, or your test subject, whether any emotions for the lamp were felt?

As the above experiment shows, the ability to read and adopt the emotions from another can happen remotely.

Remote in the sense that you may not know the person you are catching the emotions from - you need not have a pre-existing relationship with someone to have their emotions 'infect' you. Remote in the sense that you even need not be with them - you can simply observe emotions in two dimensions, on a television or a computer screen. You may well have seen the YouTube phenomenon that is Christian the Lion; try watching it without feeling generosity, goodwill and affection.

So it seems that these positive 'Blue Zone' emotions are very contagious, particularly when we observe generosity or vulnerability. As it turns out, the negative emotions associated with our Red Zone states are far more contagious, more rapid in their adoption and more persistent after the event. Something like the 'Christian the Lion' video may have a 'contagion impact' of minutes, but road rage, recalcitrant teenagers and angry customers can affect us for hours, or longer. Research suggests that Red Zone emotions are more contagious than Blue Zone emotions. Further, the greater the energy in the exchange, the greater the 'infection'. This would explain the contagiousness on one hand of Christian the Lion (with its attendant highly demonstrative affection) and, on the other, road rage.

To further add to the 'hair trigger' state that accompanies Red Zone emotions, it seems that leaders are more contagious than peers. Teachers in classrooms, bosses in boardrooms, parents with children: all are in the most 'infectious' positions.

To recall another example, think to when you were last in a classroom and the teacher used their positional power to drive towards coercive behaviour management. Imagine that you are getting on with your work, when one of the challenging students in the class causes a minor disruption. For a variety of reasons, the teacher may, themselves not be in the most ideal brain state. The outcome is as common as it is predictable: "YOU - get out of my class now!!" Let's take a moment to consider the impact on the brain and mind states immediately after this has happened.

Firstly, the challenging student will have had their own limbic activity ramped up, as a direct result of the actions of the teacher. Consequently, this student is now far less able to understand the needs and emotions of others, manage their own impulses, and track errors against values or expectations. In one simple step, their survival circuits have been switched on, and their focus is now very much on the needs of themselves, not others.

Secondly, there is a good chance that the student in question will respond back to the teacher with more Red Zone. This will have the effect of further raising the Red Zone activity of the teacher, with the outcome leading only to Red Zone Escalation.

None of this may yet be of much news to you: this is very much an everyday occurrence between two people in some way, somewhere. The real, and often hidden, impact of such a situation is on the observers. In this example, every student who witnesses the disagreement, themselves, has increased Red Zone activity. In one fell swoop, the original coercive behaviour management strategy has shifted everyone in the room into their individual Red Zones. While this will vary in degree for the individual, there will have been a collective shift from being socially interested, to being self interested. No one is, or can be, a winner here.

Such examples are not restricted to classrooms. Road rage, board room tantrums and other such overt displays of anger are a part of our every day life.

Take something recently witnessed by Andrew whilst travelling by car:

After stopping for lunch, I was in a queue for one of the 'healthy' fast food chains, that make your order in front of you. The first inkling of a problem behind the counter was the rather offhand impatience, from the sales assistant, with my hesitation in making a choice. "The menu is there, right in front of you", was inflected with enough emotion (frustration) for me to feel my feathers ruffled, so to speak. While this was a minor incident, it led me to watch further, as I ate my lunch nearby. Sure enough, a young man, unhappy with what had been made for him and, more to the point, the way he was treated around this, rather grumpily pushed back his food, and words were exchanged. Clearly, his choice was like it or lump it, and he lumped, it asking for a refund.

What happened next is possibly the worst example of customer *service that I have witnessed: the person serving him threw the refund back at the fellow, accompanied by "You shouldn't have f****ng thrown your food at me". The impact of this was immediate, not only on the customer - who responded by upending the contents of the counter on the floor - but on all who witnessed this. Anger, embarrassment and distress were rampant, and several people left the queue.*

Knowing this, particularly if you depend on the provision of a service or product, is critical. In literal terms, injury is added to insult to a degree by the rapid hard-wiring of emotional memories in our limbic systems, particularly the amygdalae. In other words, highly charged Red Zone emotions that are caught from others are sticky, and easily recalled. It is likely that, for those present, it will take some time to forget what was witnessed in that food court.

Action Zone: Red Zone Awareness

Use the list of questions here to explore the impact of your Red Zone on yourself and on others:

What do you predominantly feel when you are in your Red Zone?

What are the major physical signs that indicate that you are in your Red Zone?

What are the major or consistent triggers? (Think of when you are under pressure most)

How often do you notice that you are in your Red Zone?

How often do others notice that you are in your Red Zone?

How long do your Red Zone moments persist?

When you are in your Red Zone, what is it most of all that you take from your close relationships?

When you are in your Red Zone, what is it most of all that you take from the teams that you are a member of or lead?

How easy or difficult (1=difficult, 10=easy) is it for you to abandon a Red Zone?

How easy do you adopt the Red Zone of other significant people in your life - loved ones? - Bosses? Direct Reports?

Chapter 4

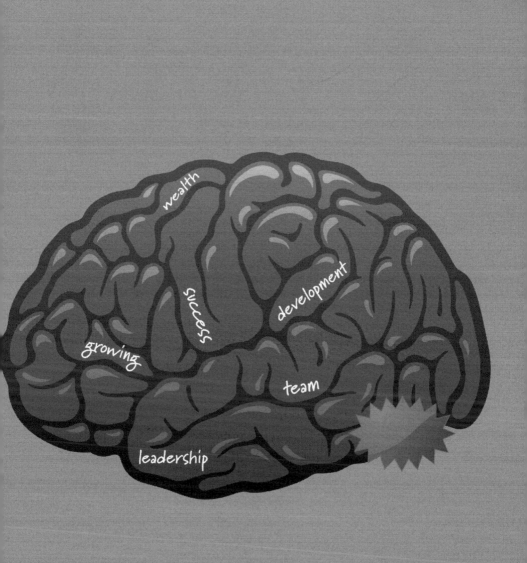

A Brain For The 21st Century

Whatever any man does he first must do in his mind, whose machinery is the brain. The mind can do only what the brain is equipped to do, and so man must find out what kind of brain he has before he can understand his own behavior.

Gay Gaer Luce and Julius Segal

One of the five key steps of the Success Zone concept is managing down the intrusion of your Red Zone into your Blue. Life presents us with many, perhaps too many opportunities for our reptilian brain to interpret a threat to our survival. Because if the reptilian brain's efficiency, the Red Zone can come to life with relative ease. This chapter illustrates habits that can be built that strongly assist in managing down your Red Zone.

Shifting From Red To Blue: Calm Under Pressure

So just as Red begets Red, Blue brings Blue. Hence, the clear message from emotional contagion research is to, at the very least, contain your own Red Zone state such that it does not transfer to others. There is a danger, here, that you will read more of fairly shortly, for as it turns out, simply *suppressing* your Red Zone state is far from sufficient. Better, a more robust alternative to responding in the Red Zone is to live strongly in the Blue. The benefits for deliberately building your ability to respond with self-awareness and self-choice are as bountiful as they are, perhaps unexpected.

Take, for example, the development of moral intelligence - as Barry Schwartz, author of Psychology of Learning and Behavior, puts it, the moral skill to know what to do and the moral will to do it. Have you ever wondered how you sourced your moral 'compass'? It seems that, rather than adopting what it is we are told we should do, we seemingly 'osmose' moral capacity from those who influence us. Consistently, the most positively influential people are those who listen, respect and believe in us. Indeed, many non-explicit 'lines of development' are grown in such a manner by an influential Blue Zone Person: social, emotional, spiritual, moral, aesthetic and values intelligences are all built this way.

> "Consistently, the most positively influential people are those who listen, respect and believe in us."

Again, using the classroom as an example, a student who experiences a Red Zone behaviour management style from the teacher will only have this reinforced as an exemplar method of engaging others. Further, building habitual Red Zone 'circuitry' in students sets them up for an adult life where change is more difficult to integrate. Rather, a student who observes a teacher staying calm under pressure has an alternate strategy presented, one that itself catalyses people towards growth. Given that many of our students come from homes and cultures where the Red Zone the norm, they may have had little, or no Blue Zone experience at all. This presents a greater imperative for our education systems to provide strong Blue Zone exposure to our emerging generations.

We would see that increasing your capacity to grow and engage yourself, and others, is dependent on two simultaneous actions: managing down the Red Zone whilst building the capacity of the Blue. We will be addressing building Blue Zone capacity later in the book, particularly around the listening and questioning capabilities.

So how do you manage down the Red Zone then? As a preliminary step towards considering strategies that help you stay calm under pressure, consider the range of methods we have at our disposal for managing emotions. After all, managing our emotions is what helps us stay calm under pressure.

How We Manage Emotions

Dr Kevin Ochsner, Director of the Centre for Cognitive Science at New York University, has been conducting and coordinating research into cognitive self regulation of emotions since 2001. His work has contributed heavily to the field of emotional regulation, and one of the purposes of this book is to leverage the outcomes of such work in a more publicly accessible format.

He suggests, firstly, thinking about something that might 'knock you off your perch' towards your Red Zone. One could categorise five mechanisms you might use to deal with the emotions that arise. These mechanisms are listed in order below in terms of the stimulus-response time line. In other words, the first is a mechanism that is employed before emotions become conscious, the fifth *after* the emotions have become evident.

1. Situation Selection

In order to avoid loss or pain, or indeed, to maximise reward, people sometimes tend to avoid or select situations that provide the desired outcome. For instance, a US study on firing behaviour of infantry in World War 2 found that some 80% of troops were deliberately firing over the heads of the enemy as a strategy for avoiding pain arising from firing at another person. This pain stemmed from conflict in values, where the limbic system could input that attempting to kill another conflicted with the orders given.

Those who fear drowning will avoid swimming, while for me, a somewhat well established fear of heights will have me avoiding bungee jumping at all costs. Equally, the brain's reward-seeking behaviour might cause you go out of your way to assist someone because (as has been shown empirically) the brain finds reward in altruism.

Seeking situations that reward and avoiding those that present pain or loss is not very adaptive in our fast-changing world. Where leadership and influence are demanded as agents of change, situation selection is a maladapted strategy.

2. Situation Modification

The US Army's response to the disturbing news that 80% of their ammunition was deliberately wasted was to build a process of drill and practice to overcome the moral dilemma. In other words, modify the situation through drill and practice such that the emotional response was bypassed. See the enemy, shoot the enemy. Thinking and feeling were largely taken out of the picture.

Similarly, someone who fears public speaking (which is, by the way the number one fear in the world) might rote learn their speech in order to modulate the fear. Confidence in knowing the content can help manage down the fear. This approach, however, only stands well where the situation remains relatively stable and predictable. Where the situation changes, say, when the projection of a PowerPoint slideshow fails, modulating the emotional response through drill and practice largely fails.

3. Distraction

Distraction is really the process of changing what it is that you are attending to. If, in presenting a public talk, I notice a particularly angry face in the crowd, it might ordinarily trigger the Red Zone *cascade* of "Oh look, he's

angry ⋯ what have I said? ⋯I'm no good at this ⋯ I want
to disappear into a hole in the ground⋯". Distraction can
be useful in this circumstance by avoiding input triggers
that upend us emotionally. As simple is this sounds, it turns
out that it takes some practice to avoid the trigger once you
notice it. We have, as humans, the irrational propensity
to engage with something, *knowing* it's negative outcome.
Rubbernecking at a road accident, smelling our hands
after we have touched something that smells disgusting, or
returning our gaze to the angry face in the crowd.

The trick is, it seems, a moment of acknowledgement,
followed by a moment of internal agreement not to engage
any further. Without the acknowledgement - "I know the
angry face is there⋯" - the internal attentional circuits
continue to press to revisit the angry face.

Studies of distraction as a strategy for managing down the
Red Zone show that it can work well in the short term, say,
for a period of up to twenty four hours, but has almost
no impact beyond this time frame. If the trigger remains,
trauma or grief for example, distraction turns out to be of
limited benefit.

4. Cognitive Modulation - Thinking about feelings

Of all the methods we have at our disposal to process
and manage emotions, thinking about feelings is the
most effective. It is a collaboration of the intelligence of
expression of our new brain, with the visceral intelligence

of our mid-brain. It is the embodiment of the Blue Zone. It is perhaps most familiar in the form articulated by the famed holocaust survivor, Victor Frankl. Through the core belief of "···nobody can take from me the way I choose to think", he was able to find meaning in living in the face of the most extreme of emotional 'injuries'.

> "Of all the methods we have at our disposal to process and manage emotions, thinking about feelings is the most effective."

Thinking about feelings includes a number of sub-strategies that we will cover shortly. Thinking about feelings builds the first pillar of the Blue Zone: awareness. Kevin Ochsner comments on this strategy by saying:
" ···(this) strategy is the one that beats all of the others in one key way: you can deploy it no matter what situation you are in and is almost universally applicable."

In supporting the Blue Zone nature of this strategy, he goes on to say:

"The ability to implement these (this strategy) depends on brain systems generally involved in the control of behaviour, and include, most importantly portions of your prefrontal cortex. ···(some are) thought to carry out specific processes associated with retrieving, maintaining and manipulating information in memory. (Other regions) are thought to be important for reasoning about the mental states of yourself and someone else. ···different combinations of regions will be recruited to support your use of it."

5. Suppression

If thinking about feelings is a powerful method for managing down your Red Zone, then suppression is the opposite. While it is probably the most common method, it stands out as being the most destructive. Again turning to cognitive neuroscience, the story being told in a variety of studies is that suppression, perhaps counter-intuitively, ramps up the activity of your amygdalae. It increases stress levels in your brain and body, and, in a perverse twist on the design of suppression, the object of your suppression leaks.

Kevin Ochsner is both succinct and insightful in this metaphor: "Emotional response suppression is like trying to close the barn door as an agitated horse is trying to get out..."

Long-term stress studies are also showing that people who use suppression regularly as a coping mechanism are more likely to suffer ill-health associated with cardio-vascular and depressive disease.

Building Your Ability To Think About Emotions

Thinking about your emotions, and the thoughts that are triggered from your emotions enlists your prefrontal cortex, the 'captain' of the Blue Zone, into the experience of feeling emotions. By this very act alone, you are shifting resources *away* from your Red Zone into the Blue. People who regularly manage down their Red Zones, in the ways illustrated below, have been shown to have smaller brain 'components' associated with negative Red Zone emotions and cascades.

Practice of the following methods will reduce your preference and reliance for using Red Zone 'circuitry'.

1. Reframing: "How else might I think about this?"

"Your worst enemy cannot harm you as much as your own unguarded thoughts."
Buddhist saying

Reappraisal is the process of changing the context or meaning around an emotional input in order to 'turn up' or 'turn down' emotions. Stopping to think about this, you may recognise that we are very good at doing this already, though perhaps not in ways most useful.

Imagine that you are about to give a briefing to a group of your staff, and as you enter the meeting room your glance rests briefly on a face in the front that is frowning. If you are prone, in some way, to lacking confidence, you may interpret this emotion as being directed at you. By engaging with this 'train of emotion' you amplify its impact on you, and the feeling of lacking confidence is turned up.

There is an alternative to this reframing negatively: by saying to yourself that this person has had a rough morning and by disassociating yourself from the Red Zone cascade that might ordinarily follow. It is about being more observational than analytical.

Try a different example: a teacher that walks into a room of students and notices two girls off task, giggling whilst looking from the teacher, to themselves. A 'vulnerable' teacher with Red Zone within easy reach might interpret and analyse the situation thus:

    These girls are not doing what they should

    They are laughing at me

    I need to assert my authority

The likely outcome is some sort of Red Zone coercive response.

    An observational teacher will simply observe: these girls are off task. This teacher will then use any number of strategies such as

    Possibly ignoring the girls

    Asking them: "Are you clear with what you have to do girls? ⋯ Anything getting in the way for you?"

    Reminding them: "The fair rule here is to allow others to work..."

Giving them a choice: "You'll need to choose, now, between getting on with the task or being separated...")
If the problem demands it, the teacher may even need support through excluding the girls short term.

The thing is, rather than allowing the analysis to drive the personalisation thought train and its resulting Red Zone Cascade, simple observation combined with clear strategy assists people in a range of professions and situations to stay calm under pressure. Effective reappraisal and reframing are very much observational in nature. Ineffective reframing is analytical, and is usually personalised in some way.

Reframing has many possibilities once you begin to see how common it is as a strategy: DeBono's Six Thinking Hats is a structured and strategic reframing process where you view or a situation or problem from the position of a single context. Each of the hats are:

Neutrality (White) - considering purely what information is available, what are the facts?
Feeling (Red) - instinctive gut reaction or statements of emotional feeling (but not any justification)
Negative judgement (Black) - logic applied to identifying flaws or barriers, seeking mismatch
Positive Judgement (Yellow) - logic applied to identifying benefits, seeking harmony

Creative thinking (Green) - statements of provocation and investigation, seeing where a thought goes
Process control (Blue) - thinking about thinking

In using reframing towards staying calm under pressure, applying each of the above perspectives to the problem allows clarity, and even insight, to emerge.

As a final example of the diversity of reframing, try to recall a situation where you, or someone else with you, was able to shift an impending conflict with a deft dab of humour. Take the following story:

A client of mine was working at a major home improvement store in the paint department. When customers have complaints, paint is the last place you want to be, since they usually discover a problem after they have already spread it on their wall. And special colours are not accepted for return. One customer got so upset at the man that he said, "You can take this paint and shove it up your ***!" The man responded, "I'm sorry sir, you're the third person to say that today so I'm all full of paint, but I'll be open for more tomorrow." The customer laughed and they were able to move on.

Some who read this story will find amusement, others might think "...how did he get away with that?". Assuming that the quip worked as indicated, what the sales assistant did was to reframe for both himself and his customer, shifting what was a Red Zone situation into very much that of the Blue

Zone. Humour, itself, is very much a Blue Zone mind state, where it seems that we can hold ambiguity in a way that does not trigger our Red Zone.

2. Acceptance and permission

"Mindfulness is the aware, balanced acceptance of the present experience."
It isn't more complicated that
It is opening to or receiving the present moment, pleasant or unpleasant, just as it is, without either clinging to it or rejecting it."
Sylvia Boorstein

This form of thinking about emotions is very much in the flavour of Buddhist philosophy. It is about unconditional acceptance for how things are now, including how I feel. Several thoughts and observations, particularly in the experiencing of negative Red Zone emotions arise from this position:

I am not defined, as a person, by how I feel
What I feel is transient - l will not always feel like this
I have a choice, no matter how inaccessible this choice might seem now, around how it is I can, should and might feel.

This recognition of the nature of human emotion is just as much permissioning as it is observation and acceptance.

People who employ this form of thinking awareness do not fight the Red Zone emotions, but simply accept them as a moment in life. By not fighting or engaging with the Red Zone in this manner, the cascade of thoughts and emotions further into the 'Red' is avoided.

3. Impartial observer

A successful therapeutic approach being employed by practitioners is the Impartial Observer technique. Take the following example by way of explanation:

You find yourself in a heated emotional exchange with someone close to you. As the exchange develops you might perhaps know that you are not necessarily thinking well. Your emotions are elevated, and your verbal responses are impulsive, not considered. Things are said on both sides of the exchange that are hurtful. It is like you are in a wrestling match, and that you are on the canvas, in the struggle. If you find yourself in this position, with minimal choice and awareness, you are in a strong Red Zone moment, perhaps even, as Daniel Goleman puts it, an 'amygdala hijack'.

When you later recall the disagreement, particularly when you recall or retell it from your perspective, all of the associated emotions painfully come to the surface. People with a strong impartial observer skill will, after the painful recall in the first person, step back from the immediacy of the experience, as if they were a spectator at the wrestling match. They will recall the exchange from this perspective, making, again, *observations* around things such as the triggers, the importance of various elements, the outcomes and possible ways forward. From this position of 'altitude' looking down as the impartial observer, reflection, clarity and insight have a much greater chance of emerging.

Having a structured set of questions can sometimes help make the switch from being in the match to observing it. Consider the following questions:

Step 1: What is the current reality? What happened? What have I seen, what have I heard? What did I do? What was done by others?

Step 2: How did/do I feel? What emotions were present then, or now?

Step 3: What have I learnt from the situation?

Step 4: What are the implications around what I have learnt?

Step 5: What can I or should I do now that I know all of this?

Often, when we relive the heat of the moment, we stay stuck in the first two steps - we do the Red Zone two step dance. Taking a strong impartial stance to the first two steps and combining this with asking the last three engages, again, your prefrontal cortex.

4. Affect labeling – naming your emotions

In many ways the simplest and quickest to implement, affect labeling is the neuroscience term for naming emotions. Matthew Lieberman, author of many elegant social neuroscience experiments at UCLA has shown, using fMRI brain scanning, that when a person experiences an emotion and labels that emotion, activity in what we would call the Red Zone decreases. It seems that, again, the internal or external languaging of an emotion enlists the Blue Zone into the mix, an act that, in and of itself, shifts resource flow to the Blue Zone.

So, simply saying to yourself "I am in the Red Zone" will go some of the way towards starting the balance shift back to the Blue Zone. As Marion has been able to demonstrate, the simple recognition of the Red Zone mind state is enough for her to wrest some choice and control out of the dominance of the Red Zone cascade.

The important thing, here, seems to be keeping the naming of the emotion succinct or symbolic. For instance, "I feel frustrated" is succinct, "I am in the Red Zone" is symbolic. The abstract nature of symbolic and succinct labeling seems, again, to force the use of Blue Zone regions of the brain.

Interestingly, a coach preparation technique called "Clearing the Space", from David Rock of Results Coaching systems, is very much an affect labeling process. This technique takes an inventory of the 'headline' issues present in the awareness of the coach and attaches an emotion to that headline. Some sort of acknowledgement of 'parking' the issue for the moment completes the process. For example, such an inventory might look like:

> I am seeing the bank manager this afternoon, I feel anxious, I'll put it aside.
>
> I have an interview for a promotion Friday, I feel nervous, I'll put it aside.
>
> I have just had a disagreement with a colleague, I feel agitated, I'll put it aside.

This works extremely well in preparing for situations that demand strong focus, such as coaching, but works equally as well in bringing clarity to the present in any context. It works best when the detail is missing, only the headline of the issue is required. It also builds emotional literacy: being able to quickly label an emotion is both a skill and an attribute of emotionally intelligent people.

Action Zone: Label Your Emotions

Take the time to put your finger on your emotional 'pulse' regularly, particularly when starting to feel the Red Zone rising. Start by recognising the Red Zone itself, then develop finesse by more accurately labeling the emotion. The resources page of our website (http://www. thesuccesszone.com/resources) has a list of commonly felt emotions to help your limbic literacy if you have trouble identifying how you feel.

As a final word on labeling emotions, we put the question to Matthew Lieberman: "If labeling negative emotions moderates them, does the same happen when we label positive emotions?". His answer was both warning and observation:

"Indeed yes, if positive emotions are labeled then it seems we feel them less. Strangely, people tend to say when they are feeling good and ignore labeling when it is a negative emotion. Perhaps we have this the wrong way around..."

Pain And Reward In The Social Brain

By now, you should have a strongly emerging picture of the Blue and Red Zone mind states. As a closing piece to this chapter, we would like you to consider the impact of social and emotional pain in the brain. If nothing else, this should convince you that understanding the impact of the emotional brain is now hard, not soft science. Neuroscience, amongst many recent contributions to our world, has at last given real cause for leadership to pay attention to things emotional.

Matthew Lieberman has teamed with Naomi Eisenberger around the question "···how is a broken heart like a broken leg". They had both noted the striking observation that "...the language we use to describe social pain is in fact the language of physical pain." This led to an investigation of the pain and reward systems in the brain, in terms of both the physical and social domains. What they have found is as curious as it is significant.

Pain

When self-reported discomfort is measured against physical pain, two regions of the brain show increased activity: the dorsal anterior cingulate cortex (dACC) and the right ventro-lateral prefrontal cortex (RVLPFC). These are significant areas of the 'human' or cortical brain. More important than the names or locations themselves, Lieberman and Eisenberger found , when they measured self-reported social pain from exclusion, a very strong correlation with the same brain regions. Social pain was also activated in the dACC and the RVLPCF. These findings have been replicated, with a number of interesting outcomes:

A double blind test for paracetamol found that it was able to mediate social pain in much the same way, though not to the same degree, as it does physical pain. Equally, some of the drugs associated with social pain, Prozac for instance, have been shown to moderate physical pain.

Individuals, who have a higher tolerance for physical pain, seem also to have a greater tolerance to social pain.

According to Lieberman and Eisenberger, it may well be that the social pain system may have piggybacked onto the physical pain system during mammalian evolution [Esienberger & Lieberman 2004, Panksepp 1998], "...borrowing the pain signal to indicate broken social bonds". Importantly, this research powerfully suggests that social pain both real and significant in its manifestation in the brain and 'the person'.

Reward

'The Ultimatum Game' has become a foundation tool in the search for answers in social cognitive neuroscience. In its basic form, this game provides that two individuals split a sum of money between them. The proposer offers a way to split the money, while the responder chooses whether, or not, to accept. If the offer is accepted, both players receive what was proposed. If rejected, both players receive nothing.

On the outset, this would seem simple beyond use. The rational in us would say, that regardless of any offer, the responder will be in front with any split, even if it was only, say one dollar out of ten. The thing is, though, that *fairness*, a social and emotional measure, is perceived. When this fairness element is detected, and evaluated in fMRI scans, a region of the brain called the ventral striatum is activated. This is a major part of the brain's reward system, and is also activated with physical reward.

Again, studies of other aspects of social reward, including positive social feedback, donating and altruism continue to show that the reward centre is activated in these circumstances. Some studies are showing that the brain responds more to social reward, as such, than, say, financial reward.

Conclusion

The consideration of how social pain and reward impacts on us further supports the model of the Blue and Red Zones. Simple 'carrot and stick' methods of change remain inefficient and, at best, short-term change agents given that they engage the Red Zone more than the Blue. People, like your best teachers or leaders, have a high impact on others because they engage the Blue Zone in a manner that triggers our social reward systems. The chapters that follow, now, are much more around putting this into action.

Action Zones: The Four Ways of Thinking About Emotions

1. Take a moment to think about the list above. Which do you do 'natively', which might be less natural to you?

Now think for a moment about a recent challenging situation, one where your Red Zone was very much engaged.

For example, recently at an airport Andrew had his carry-on bag scanned six times. "This put me last onto the plane, and caused me to have to place my bag overhead away from where I was sitting. I knew that this was going to make life getting off the plane more difficult than I needed. I wanted to let the person checking my bag know about how his need to re-scan so many times had impacted on me, but sitting in a plane in the air, I couldn't."

In recalling your thoughts and feelings for your example, consider the questions against each of the techniques: Labeling: What feelings did I have, in one or two words?

Acceptance: What thoughts could I have had that might have allowed me to accept the situation?

Reframing: How else might I have been able to interpret this situation?

Impartial Observer: If I was a fly on the wall, what insights might I gain from my distance?

2. Given that life presents us with a rich and diverse array of Red Zone triggers, pick one trigger that you know will be persistent or regular and use it to practice one of the four methods of staying cool under pressure. For best results early in this process, choose a Red Zone trigger that is transient rather than something that has been affecting you for some time.

Choose the method that you are natively strong in, and deliberately apply it to the trigger. Watch how you respond to the trigger over a period of time, remembering that it takes the adult brain six to twelve weeks to permanently hardwire a habit with repetitive attention.

It may help to rate the degree and persistence of your Red Zone response early in the process of practicing staying cool under pressure. Every week or so, take a snapshot of your response 'vitals' to see how you are progressing. We have also found it helpful to have others provide feedback on how they see your response in terms of degree and persistence of visible Red Zone indicators.

Once you feel you have habituated a Blue Zone counter to Red Zone triggers using one of the techniques, move onto one of the others.

3. For more deep-seated Red Zone situations that could be improved with a building of your capacity in some way, try applying the REACH set of questions.

Note that the final question deals with what action you are going to take - the beauty of this set of questions lies in the circular nature of their application.
In other words, the action you take becomes the subject of the first question the next time you go through the REACH framework. (The full REACH framework is shown in the appendix.)

Step 1: What is the current Reality? What happened? What have I seen, what have I heard? What did I do? What was done by others?

Step 2: What Emotions do I have? How did/do I feel? What emotions were present then, or now?

Step 3: What have I Acquired from the situation?

Step 4: What Connections can I make? What are the implications around what I have learnt?

Step 5: What Happens next? What can I or should I do now that I know all of this?

Next Steps: Blue Zone Organisations

A significant next step that you can take, in assisting an organisation to move forward, is to educate people about their own Blue and Red Zones, along with the impact of these two mind states. Being a concept that 'lands' with people, and is 'sticky' in its language, we have found that young primary school students all the way through to leaders of organisations adopt and use the language quickly.

Once the mind states are in place and the ideas are understood, the concept of Blue and Red Zones can be used to frame how people might behave and interact within an organisation. While schools are obvious candidates for such a framework, any organisation that demands growth and learning, and where interaction between its people impacts on the outcomes of the organisation, can benefit.

Applying the steps and skills outlined in this book to the leadership group alone has been shown to reliably shift an organisation into being a Blue Zone Organisation.

Chapter 5

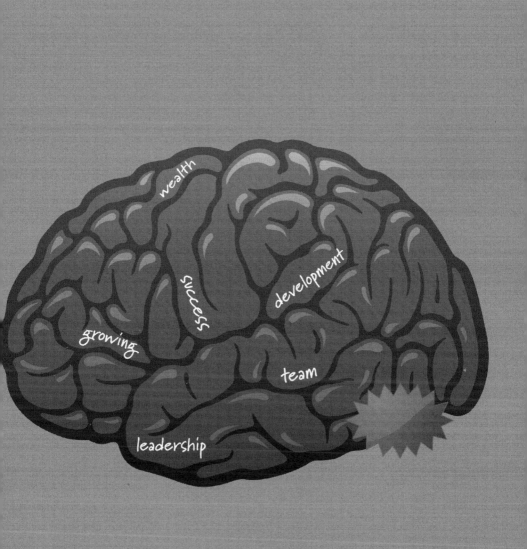

Powerful Questioning

"Socrates, you will remember, asked all the important questions - but he never answered any of them"

Dickson Richards

True learning, whether self-directed or catalysed by the influence of another, emerges from reflection, clarity and insight. Have you ever stopped to consider that, as an adult, when nearly all of our biological systems are in slow decline, the only aspect of ourselves that can continue to grow is that of our mind. Questions, then, become powerful tools of growth, creating the 'mind-space' from which reflection, clarity and insight can emerge. Questions also have the inherent potential to direct particular brain regions to become active. Through this potential, questions can become potent instruments for fostering and habituating the use of the Blue Zone.

For most of us, the way that we question has been learnt, but not taught. Just like we learn to walk, but are most often never taught, both the method and the questions we use are 'osmosed' from those around us. This means that we have a default questioning skillset is rarely questioned for how effective it might be. We have little understanding of the impact on others of the questions we use, and even whether the questions are really more for us, or for them.

"This means that we have a default questioning skillset, that itself, is rarely questioned for how effective it might be."

Your Default Questions

Before reading any further, let's check in on what questions you have 'at hand'. Imagine that a colleague is really under pressure at work, and has begun to talk to you about how busy and stressed they are, and that the task load that they have just seems to be growing and growing.

"I'm so stressed at the moment, and my to-do list just seems to be growing and growing"

Take a few moments (and using a sheet of paper and a pen), write down what questions you could ask this colleague to help them in some way with their frustration. Time yourself for five minutes to see how many questions come to mind.

We'll come back to looking more closely at what you have developed as a list of questions in a moment. Just for now, reflect on the origin of your questions: From where did this repertoire of questions develop? For many of us, there has been no explicit and deliberate development of our ability to ask the best questions. Rather, we just ask what is obvious (to us) to ask.

Returning to the list of questions you have created: we would like you to exclude some on the basis that they may not be as useful as you might think in helping your colleague reflect, find clarity and discover insight. Taking a close look at your list, firstly exclude anything that might suggest, even subtly, advice or action in some way. Such questions might look like:

> "Have you thought of time management?"
> "How would prioritising help here?"
> "I wonder if you should try yoga?"
> "Why don't you try delegating?"

The next group of questions to exclude are those that direct the attention of your colleague towards the "less stressed" part of the statement. This tends to be one of the two obvious things to ask about, yet, as counter intuitive as it might seem, paying close attention at this point to what might be causing stress, or what might remove stress, may not be as helpful as you think. Hence, for the moment, exclude anything like:

> "What things are causing you most stress?"
> "What would your day be like without stress?"
> "What helps you keep calm?"

Note that, while this last question does not directly address the issue of stress, it still draws the coachee's attention to 'stress'.

The last group of questions to exclude, using the same logic as excluding questions around stress, are questions that focus on 'the tasks' that keep piling up. Exclude, then, anything that might sound like:

"What tasks are getting in the way for you?"

"Which tasks are the most important to do first?"

"Are there any tasks that you might delegate?"

Often we find that after excluding the above three groups of questions, many people have only a few, if any, questions that have escaped the cull. This may have left you pondering what is left to ask? We'll come to answer this soon, but before we do that, it is worth pausing to consider two question traps: assumption and detail.

Assumption – A Hidden Trap

Consider, for a moment, a trivia question we found a few years ago in a local newspaper: "Who am I? I have won more Oscars than anyone else in history." This becomes interesting and relevant here only if you do not know the answer.

Who comes to mind for you? Do you see their face, or do you think of their name?

We use this to illustrate the point that our mind does something extremely well - it builds associations through your neural networks, and starts to present some options for you. The thing is, this ability to make assumptions and to create options, as useful as it is in most circumstances, can very much get in the way.

Were you thinking of someone classic like Katherine Hepburn? Perhaps John Wayne? The next clue in the six-step 'who am I' question was "My first character appeared on screen towards the end of the 1920s." How does this change your thinking?

Indeed, the answer is not an actor or actress. Those of you who perhaps thought, in the first instance, of Stephen Spielberg, were on the right track, for it was Walt Disney.

The point here, is that as long as you hold the assumption that the answer is an actor or actress, you cannot get the correct answer. Note that the first clue did not mention the word actor, your strong associative neural maps connected Oscar with actor for you. Information that was not actually in the original clue.

How does this relate to effective questioning? When you hear from someone the words "I'd love to be less stressed, but the tasks just keep piling up ⋯" your neural maps kick in, particularly if you have had this experience yourself. You fill in the gaps for this person, and assume that the statement *actually* means that the issue surrounds task management and stress.

This assumption, then, would drive the sorts of questions that you might ask, focusing on the almost-blinking words of stress and tasks. For example, "Which tasks are causing you stress?" or "Have you thought of prioritising your tasks?". Both of these questions are in easy reach of our default repertoire. Yet, by asking these questions, we corral the thinking of the person to consider *only* stress and tasks.

If we ask a different question, one with no assumptions embedded, then the coachee may well consider the issue differently: *"If things were perfect tomorrow in terms of your stress and task load, what would be different for you?"*. Instead of being confined to conventional and expected answers, the coachee here might say "I'd be more confident in my role". This 'left field' answer, which may, in fact, be an insight for the coachee, was enabled by asking a question with no boundaries.

> "If things were perfect tomorrow in terms of your stress and task load, what would be different for you?"

Powerful questions, ones that elicit reflection, clarity and insight, are not underpinned by assumption, nor do they impose containment on thinking.

One very useful model for thinking, for knowing the best questions to ask and for shaping conversations that grow, is the 'skyscraper' model:

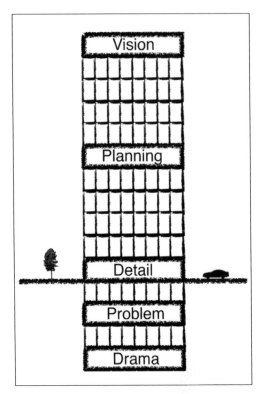

The higher up this model our thinking and speaking is, the further we can see, the greater clarity we have, the greater the chance for insight. Unfortunately for many of us, our default question repertoire tends to address thinking and speaking at the detail level and below. Being on the 'ground floor' as we are when we consider detail, we tend only to see what is in front of us, both in terms of events, information and time.

The Devil *IS* In The Detail

Asking questions about the detail in a dilemma is both easy and comfortable: we can see what the detail is, we can avoid uncomfortable periods of silence and we can even contribute solutions from the details that we might have to the other person. Sadly, all of these get in the way of the other person growing, of them finding their own solution.

Noteworthy is the point that, most often, what we ask for is what we get. If we ask for detail, we get it; if we ask an attacking answer we get a defensive answer; if we ask about what someone is thinking, they tell us what they are thinking. The potential for growth, or at least a significant part of this potential, lies in the nature of the question we ask.

Let's return, then, to the questions that you eliminated in the earlier exercise. Try mapping these against the 'skyscraper' model: do you notice that most, if not all of your excluded questions fit against *Detail, Problem* or *Drama?* You should see, equally, that the surviving questions are most likely ones that address *Vision* and/or *Planning.*

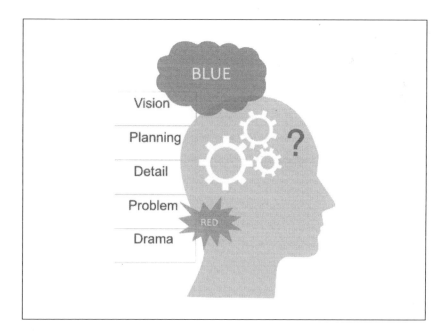

The idea should now be emerging for you: one of the secrets

of growth is to ask the best questions for growth.

Questions For Growth

Recall, for a moment, that adaption, growth and lasting learning all are strongly seated in the Blue Zone. Hence, it would be requisite that the questions we use for growth would hold another person in their Blue Zone. The best questions will trigger reflection, clarity and insight. It is worth noting here that the questions that spark reflection, clarity and insight borrow heavily from the field of coaching.

Time, then, to take a deeper look at what makes a great question for growth. In this exercise, take a moment to recall a situation, recent if you can, where things did not go as well as they should. Perhaps it was not following up with a client, an out of control argument with your partner or an event you planned that crashed and burned.

We'd like you to apply two sets of questions against this event, to see what effect each question set has on your thinking and feeling. If you can, grab another person, someone you feel comfortable with, and have them ask you these questions:

SET 1:
Why didn't you perform as you should?
Why did this happen?

Where did it all start to go wrong?
Why do you think that you are no good at this?
Why did you do it that way?

Take a moment to measure how you feel, and what style of thinking response you had. If you had another person ask you these questions, check with them to see how they felt asking these questions. Most people report that these questions cause the reliving of the negative feelings surrounding the event, that both the thinking and answers are defensive, and that they feel stuck and hopeless. So, remembering that there is a strong link between what we ask and what we get back, what is present in the questions above that cause such responses?

It turns out that the two most destructive elements of the questions above are a focus on the problem (I feel stuck) and an opinion (I feel judged). Indeed, it is the latter that causes a Red Zone response, even when opinion (or judgement, or advice) is only subtly present in the question. Problem-focused questions, on their own, are not the issue: identifying the problem can be a useful, if not necessary, part of the process. However, the repetition of the problem focus is a problem in the above question set.

An alternative then? Try asking yourself (or having your buddy ask) the next set of questions:

SET 2:
What aspects of this situation are you happy with?
What did you learn from this particular situation?
How would you rate your effectiveness here, say, out of 10?
What rating would you be pleased with?
What do you need to do to move towards your preferred rating?
What will you do now that you know this?

Again, take a moment to reflect on the impact of these questions. What did you notice? If you had a partner ask you these questions, how did they feel? Most people report that they feel energised, optimistic and in control, usually because there has been some non-judgemental acknowledgement and some move towards a solution. Try looking for evidence of opinion, judgement and advice in the second set of questions. Indeed, the questions are 'clean' of these destructive elements - it would be very hard to discern anything of the thinking of the questioner. These questions also focus on how things are now, or how they could be in the future.

Have you noticed another difference? See how 'why' is common in the first set, and absent in the second? 'Why' questions are very hard to ask without any risk of the 'interviewee' interpreting judgement. Further, 'why' questions direct attention towards problem and defense. Consider the usefulness of an answer (to either person) when you ask a why question. Think of when you last asked a child "Why did you hit your brother?" or "Why did you break that toy?" or "Why are you home late?"··· Often, the why question is rhetorical and code for 'I am not happy'.

Asking The Best Questions

Summarising the key points here, we would say that:

Questions are a linguistic tool for directing attention - repetitively directing attention to the problem will trigger more of a Red Zone response, attention to the solution will cause the Blue Zone to be activated.

Questions that begin with 'why', and have any of the thinking of the asker present (opinion, judgement or advice) will also trigger the Red Zone.

Questions that address Detail, Problem or Drama will also typically activate the Red Zone, Vision and Planning questions bias the activity in the brain toward the Blue Zone.

So how is it that you can re-wire your communication habits to use better questions? One way is to undertake some coaching training, either as a workplace coach, or towards becoming an independent coach and running your own coaching practice.

More simply, all you need do is make sure that you ask questions for growth on a regular basis. To illustrate this point, think of the person that you know that can just pull out joke after joke. Often, you will hear others say to such a person "How is it that you can remember so many jokes?" The 'brain's answer to this is that they tell lots of jokes: tell a joke three to four times in a short period of time and it becomes hard-wired into the joke repertoire. Equally, once you begin to use questions for growth more regularly, they become hard-wired into your question repertoire. Once this happens, you have a whole new potential to assist those around you to develop.

To develop this idea further, imagine that you have a colleague very much in their Red Zone, 'blowing off' about one of their peers. A question that might be close at hand for many leaders is "So why do you think this is happening?" Result? The colleague *reengages* with the emotion and the detail of the problem, further ramping up the Red Zone. Given that resolution can only come from the Blue Zone, the question above turns out to be pretty poor in assisting your colleague to move forward.

The world of coaching has been getting this right for some time now: a coach might ask "If things were as good as they can be tomorrow, what would be different?" This sort of question lifts the thinking state of the direct report out of the 'Red' into the 'Blue' because it demands reflection. While success is never guaranteed, using questions that direct attention to the present or future, not the past, is a key here. For example, simply asking "On a scale from 1 to 10, how would you rate how angry you are now?", perhaps followed by "On the same scale, how important is this issue amongst all the things you are facing now?", are good current reality questions. For most people, these questions will cause activity in the prefrontal cortex, the Blue Zone, cleverly shifting the balance away from the Red Zone.

Coaching has much to inform leadership, particularly around the language of questioning. Knowing the right questions to ask that help direct the thinking of another towards reflection and solution, for example. Unfortunately, most questions that come to mind for leaders, by default are problem or detail focused, and are not particularly helpful.

Learning some coaching questions can very much lift the effectiveness and influence of leaders when conflict comes to town.

Action Zone: Re-wiring Your Question Repertoire

Part of the process of re-wiring your habitual problem and detail-focused questions is to begin asking different questions. Recalling the previous analogy where someone you know can tell lots of jokes: each time a joke is recounted, it cements itself further into long term memory. Equally, when a joke has not been recalled for a while, the natural neuroplastic state of the brain results in synapses being pruned, and becomes less accessible. Similarly, if you want to create a new question language state, you need to ask more of the solutions-focused questions found here, and in coaching generally.

A word on doing this: most people are aware when you begin to ask different questions. If you begin to 'quasi-coach' people without their blessing, there is a danger that you will trigger their Red Zone. If you intend to ask more than one 'thinking' question, bring some clarity with it by checking in with the other person. Useful ways of doing this include:

"Do you mind if I ask you a few coaching (or thinking) questions?" (great for a quick or basic conversation)

"Do you mind if I practice my coaching on you?" (better if the conversation needs to be more formal or structured)

Key Question Types

Try using questions from the groups below in conversations where the other person is seeking clarity or insight.

The "*Miracle*" Question:
If things were perfect tomorrow (with regard to the issue at hand), what would you see or feel that is different to today?

This question type has many forms, and can be adapted to almost any context, or indeed, age. It is a perfect instance of a *vision* question.

In a startling example of how powerful this question can be, a good friend of ours from Durham, Alison, used this question with her then five year old daughter. School had reported that Alison's daughter was socially 'out of sorts', and was apportioning blame to separation anxiety, with a forthcoming trip for Alison. Indeed, Alison knew better, and asked her daughter "If school could be perfect tomorrow, how would it be different?" Immediately her daughter said "Chloe would be friends with me..." A single question, yet such clarity from a five year old. Ask yourself this question when you are lacking clarity, focus or satisfaction and see if you can find some 'instant clarity'.

Rating Questions:

How would you rate your satisfaction/effectiveness/ability (or other appropriate attribute) with regard to the issue at hand?

Rating questions are very effective at engaging the mammalian brain. Watch the other person when you ask this question. If this is, indeed, a new question to them, watch the thinking on their face! They will more than likely not go through a rational or logical analysis, but will pause, seemingly not think of anything, but access a 'best estimate', gut-feel answer. Indeed, you are assisting them to access answers held in their mammalian brain. In this, if not overused, rating questions are extremely effective.

For example:
How would you rate your current delegation effectiveness?
Follow-up rating examples (use in combination with the first):

What rating would you be happy with?
What rating do you need to meet the current challenge?
What rating would assist you to meet your goals?
What rating would be a stretch for you?

Thinking Questions:

Often we are seduced by the obvious detail in an issue or conversation. A useful group of questions that can keep you above the detail are thinking questions. Questions like:
How important is this to you?
Would it be in your top ten, top five or even top three issues?
How long have you been thinking about it?
How often do you think about it?
How is your current thinking impacting on outcomes or results?
What thinking do you need to have to meet your goal(s)?

Thinking questions, in our opinion, should always follow any information such as a suggestion (when you absolutely have no choice but to offer 'advice'), feedback or challenging information. For instance, if a person is genuinely stuck in their thinking, and you need to give them something to kick-start their cognition, it can be helpful to offer two or three options. One of these options may be something that you would like them to consider. The suggestions you make have far greater value when you follow them with: "What thinking does that trigger in you?"

This single question forces the other person to consider, make sense of and map into their world the best of the alternatives (for them) that you have offered. This may not, indeed, have been your preference, but the outcome of re-starting the thinking has been achieved. We use this question all of the time when we provide something new, different or challenging.

Feeling Questions:

The danger in asking feeling questions revolves around the level of *detail* in asking someone to recall or label an emotion. 'Detail' feeling questions tend to cause the emotion to re-resonate, with a possible return to a Red Zone state. If this occurs, the style of thinking returns to justification and defense, both of which are blockers to adaptation and growth.

It seems, certainly from what neuroscience is telling us, that asking for abstract or symbolic descriptions of emotions works best, as described in Chapter 4. Thus, asking someone to rate their feeling, to succinctly label the emotion in one word, or to use Red Zone descriptors assists them to manage down any Red Zone intrusion. Such questions also allow a person to view their emotions from the distance of the cognitive brain, allowing for clarity and insight.

Examples include:
How would you rate the intrusion of your Red Zone at the

moment, say as a score out of 10?

What one word would you use to describe you feeling?

What analogy or metaphor might you use to describe your feelings? (You might want to start them on the track with this one by adding "It feels like ⋯" and let them finish the sentence).

When addressing questions to emotions or feelings, we think it essential to move from the current state of emotions to some sort of desired state, as expressed by the speaker. Take the example where the person you are listening to says "⋯ oh I don't know, I just feel so pessimistic about my chances for promotion⋯". How often do we respond by saying "Don't feel like that - you'll be fine!"? While our intentions are clear, the impact of such a statement does not at all match the aim. The other person rarely, if ever, feels better just because we told them to. A far more effective response, by way of illustrating this point, is to ask:

"How would you prefer to feel?"

"How do you need to feel to be successful?"

"What do you need to do to be able to feel this way?"

So take the opportunity to rewire yourself to use solutions-focused questions that ignite the thinking spark for the other person. Be the catalyst that causes the Blue Zone to blossom for them through reflection, dreaming, imagination, clarity and insight.

For a more extensive resource list of questions for growth, please visit http://www.thesuccesszone.com/resources

Chapter 6

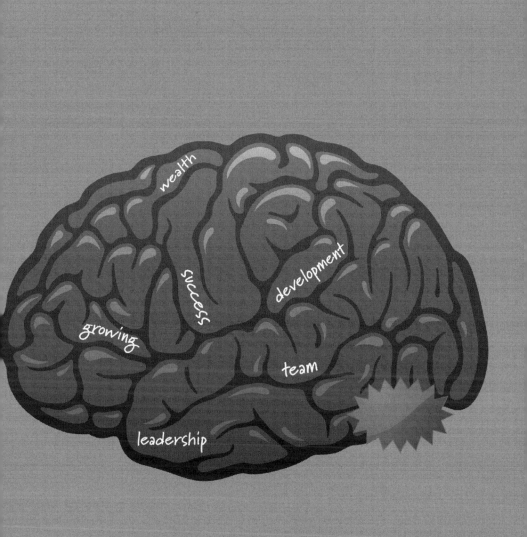

Powerful Questioning

"The most precious gift we can offer others is our presence. When mindfulness embraces those we love, they will bloom like flowers."

Thich Nhat Hanh (Vietnamese Monk, Activist and Writer)

"Listening is the currency of change: without it there would be no learning."

Andrew Mowat

If you are the moon, and a friend or colleague (who is, right at this moment, speaking) the sun, then you have two choices: to add to their world by reflecting, or to eclipse their world by moving across their thinking and feeling with your agenda.

> **"This chapter will show you that listening is as much attitude as it is skill, and that it is the X-factor of the most influential people on the planet."**

This chapter has the potential to change everything for you. Understanding the place of listening in respectful, developmental relationships is key: where knowing the right questions provides the best language tools, listening is the social mechanism that results in engagement. Highly developed listening skills correlate to high Blue Zone functioning: the best listeners are highly self-aware, and are able to manage their thoughts and impulses. This chapter will show you that listening is as much attitude as it is skill, and that it is the (often hidden) X-factor of the most influential people on the planet.

The Most Influential People
Take a moment to list the most positively influential people, that you have/had a direct relationship with (both past and present), in your life. People who have helped you grow in some way. Aim for naming five to ten people, writing them below if you will.

_____ __/10 __/10
_____ __/10 __/10
_____ __/10 __/10
_____ __/10 __/10
_____ __/10 __/10
_____ __/10 __/10
_____ __/10 __/10
_____ __/10 __/10
_____ __/10 __/10
_____ __/10 __/10

For each name, write down two scores (out of ten): one for how much respect *this person gives/gave you* and the second for how well you think that they have listened to you. What insights arise for you here? Most people who end up on such a list generally have respect and listening scores between seven and ten out of ten. We are yet to see a person named in this exercise who rates below six for either. So what does this suggest?

In our training, we often come across references to public figures that leave a strongly positive emotional 'footprint' after very brief encounters. Past US President Bill Clinton is one example that comes to mind: people often refer to his listening skills as having left them with the feeling that they were the only person in the room. The clue in his example, and in the people that you named as most influential to you, is that most of the 'attention budget' of the listener is actually being devoted to listening.

To take the opposite stance, let's see what happens emotionally when we detect that we are not being listened to. Use the list of examples below to trigger memories of similar situations for you. Sit with the memory for a while, and tap into what feelings were present for you.

You want to discuss an important concern with your line manager, and he divides his attention between you and finishing an email on his Blackberry.

You come home from work, and want to talk about a tough day, yet your partner does not stop what they were doing. When you were introduced to someone, and they kept getting your name wrong, even after several corrections. A teacher, when you have said that you don't understand, continues to tell you to read the textbook.

Not surprisingly, there is a strong link between not being listened to, not being respected or acknowledged and triggering feelings of frustration, disappointment and anger. Just as much as listening is a form of social inclusion, not being listened to is a form of social rejection, a state that we are particularly sensitive to and that is a common Red Zone trigger.

Listening Is Learnt, Not Taught

Listening, then, is a skill of attending to others, not yourself. Consider successfully hitting a golf ball: even professional golfers, who have hard-wired their muscle memory to successfully execute the swing, must attend to the ball through the moment of the swing. If attention at this critical time drifts, so too will the success of the shot. Very, very few people can achieve a successful golf shot without years of paying attention to developing the hard-wired habits of swinging. Many, if not most of us, have repeated, over time, a less than efficient golf swing, resulting in a less than ideal outcome.

> "Listening, then, is a skill of attending to others, not yourself."

As with the hacker's game of golf, the way most of us have developed our listening skills has been without strategy, knowledge or coaching. This means for most of us, we are not aware of either the explicit purpose or the subject of our listening.

Given this organic growth in listening capability, it is not surprising to know that most people tend not to be aware of the object or purpose of their listening. We just listen. Underneath this blindness (or should this be deafness) to purpose and object, the brain is paying strategic and deliberate attention to any number of things. We first became aware of this through David Rock's work, and the list below is adapted from his book 'Quiet Leadership'. It is a list of a range of different listening purposes, and as you read this list, see if you can make some observations about the dominant style of listening that you use, and that people around you at work, or home use:

- For opportunities to sound intelligent
- For a chance to say something funny
- For how I could sound important
- To information I want
- To external distractions – other noise, music etc
- For what's going on for the other person
- For approval
- To my own thoughts, not listening to the other person at all
- To be able to understand the problem
- For how I can benefit
- For the opportunity to one-up the other person
- For the details so that I can help solve the problem

- For how I can undermine the other person's point of view or position
- For how I can change or end the conversation

So which styles resonate with you as ones you use at work, or socially? What about your peers, colleagues and leaders - how do you interpret their listening purpose?

To understand the dynamics of your attention when you listen, let's just dissect one of the listening purposes a little further. Take the style of looking for 'the chance to say something funny or amusing', a common social listening style. Think of when you do this, or think of a person who you know that does this.

At first, this person will not be saying much, but will be listening to the content of the conversation. As they listen to the content, they will be mapping this content against possibilities: puns, observations, anecdotes or jokes. Once this person has found something amusing to add, they generally stop listening to the content and begin listening for the opportunity, the gaps in the conversation when intervening is socially acceptable. If a timely opportunity arises, then the amusing content is inserted, and the process is repeated. If the opportunity disappears, and the content changes, socially adept users of this style will drop their current 'potential contribution' and will start the process again, listening to the content to find something funny to add. People who are less socially agile with this style will hang on to what it is that they wish to say, adding it in spite of it no longer being funny.

The key insights, here, are that we listen with strategic intent (even when we are not aware of it), and that we are not as much listening to people as to what they are saying, and for the gaps for us to say something. Moreover, knowing that we have something that we want to say is often felt as a strong urge that directs our attention away from people to the social gaps in the conversation. Think of when you were last at a party, where a circle of people were in anecdote mode: where everyone is either just telling their story, or waiting for their turn to tell their story. Very little listening to others is occurring here!

To make one final, but critical, point here, return your attention to the list of listening purposes above. What element, common to nearly all of the purposes, do you notice in this list? Me, I, my. Most, if not all of our ways of listening are geared towards what 'I' need. Without us really being aware, we have learnt to listen, by default, in a variety of ways that serve us, the listener. Yet, we have already established in this chapter that the most influential and charismatic people listen to others, less themselves. To shape this X-factor of influence a little further now, we can say that engagement and influence is high when we detect that someone is listening to us for us, and less when we detect them listening to us for them.

"Engagement and influence is high when we detect
that someone is listening to us *for us,* and less when
we detect them listening to us *for them.*"

To illustrate the validity of this, check to see if any of the
experiences below make sense to you:

A car salesman listens, asks questions and establishes
your needs, wants and desires, or, a car salesman tries
to convince or steer you towards a car that he thinks
you need, or that he needs to move.

A doctor consults with you on a procedure, and asks
you about any questions, fears or goals you might
have, or a doctor gives you information and strong
advice about what to do next.

Legal assistance (lawyer, legal aid practitioner, etc),
that listens to your needs, seems to know you well,
and works towards your desired outcomes or legal
assistance that relies on their expertise and position to
move to a successful result in spite of your needs and
desired outcomes.

A wedding photographer that contributes to a couple
feeling like the wedding day is *their* day, or a wedding
photographer that strongly expresses the attitude of "I
am the artist/expert" in their work.

Each of these illustrates the difference between listening "to you for you", and listening "to you for me". Studies in a variety of contexts continue to show the success of the former. Indeed, one of our own studies into the legal aid system in England showed that clients were far more satisfied when they had a legal aid practitioner that knew them, their needs and desires, and that listened to them, for them. This satisfaction persisted even in the face of an unsuccessful legal outcome. Equally, those clients that experienced a satisfactory outcome, but had a legal aid practitioner that did not listen well, reported much lower levels of satisfaction. Often lower than the satisfaction levels of unsuccessful, but listened-to, clients. Attitude and behaviour rule supreme over outcome.

So how can we move from a listening purpose for ourselves, to one where we are focused much more on the 'other person'? Part of the answer is to first know *where* your attention is being 'spent' and then to make some active choices about *how* you attend. We have identified two listening styles that allow this to be hard-wired into day-to-day listening habit: *observational* and *optimistic* listening.

Action Zone: Observing Your Listening Styles

Spend some time observing your own preferred listening styles, and those of people around you. Begin to sense when it is that you, or others, are listening more for the conversational gaps than the conversation, or the person.

Chapter 7

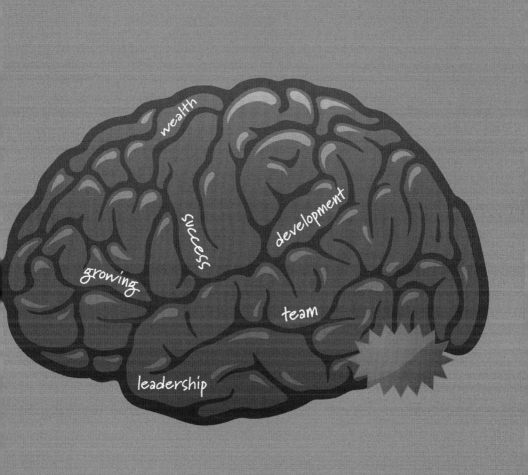

Observational Listening

"Listening is a magnetic and strange thing, a creative force. When we really listen to people there is an alternating current, and this recharges us so that we never get tired of each other. We are constantly being re-created."

Brenda Ueland (American feminist and author 1891-1985)

Observational Listening

In our cortex, that which we earlier named the human brain, we are very well endowed with complex and powerful deductive, analytical and pattern-recognising architecture. This circuitry, for most people, tends to heavily influence our listening: when we listen we seek to interpret and understand, to match to past patterns and to process the detail towards coming up with our own opinions, advice and solutions. All of this work uses a great deal of the brain's available bandwidth, and reduces the attention available to really listen to the other person. All of this processing also underpins 'listening to you, for me' - you are giving me information for me to process.

You will now be at least beginning to see that when we listen, we tend to do so with a great deal of our own thinking. To illustrate this, try the following exercise, either when you are next listening in a conversation, or by deliberately finding a partner to share in completing this exercise.

Action Zone: Observational Listening Exercise - Part 1

Choose an engaging conversation with another person, and observe yourself over a five-minute period, as you are in the conversation. A good conversation to provide some self-observation is where you ask your conversational partner to talk about a work issue that they would love to have resolved.

As you listen, write down the following things:

Thoughts about things you would like to say, or that you do say.
Other thoughts that you have that are not related to what you want to say (eg judgements, opinions etc).

What did you find emerging? Look at the list of common outcomes to this exercise and check this off against your notes:

Thoughts that are judging (e.g. "Gee, that attitude is a bit harsh ...")
Thoughts that are fitting or matching what is being heard into your own experience (e.g. "That is so what happens to me too ...")
Thoughts that are making assumptions (e.g. Finishing sentences, "I know where this is going ...")
Thoughts that trigger processing (trying to solve the problem, distracting thoughts, going off into another thought train ...)

Nearly always, when we work with people through this exercise, we find that the listener engages with at least one, if not all of these internal thoughts. The insight for many is "Gosh, how busy is my brain when I am listening!". The thing is, *none of the above* is helpful for either the speaker or the listener if engagement, empathy or influence are desired outcomes.

To get a sense of the alternative listening state, try the second part to this exercise:

Action Zone: Observational Listening Exercise - Part 2

Choose another listening opportunity, or continue the deliberate conversation you have had with a partner about a work issue that they would love to have resolved. If this is an opportunistic (rather than deliberate) conversation, it may well help to say "I am practicing a different listening style - do you mind if I use this as an opportunity to develop my listening skills?"

This time, listen to them with the pure and express purpose of feeding back to them what you hear, see and observe.
Let the other person speak uninterrupted for at least 2 minutes, and when they have finished, relate back to them your observations. If this is a deliberate conversation to experience this exercise, then taking notes will assist you here.

Things you may want to watch for:
• Words that are stressed or emphasised in some way

- Body language - hand movements, body position, expressions (fleeting or persistent)
- Voice characteristics (speed, pitch)
- Thinking or feelings that you observe

What are your insights from this exercise? What did the speaker notice from being given uninterrupted space to talk? Did they notice an absence of advice, judgement or assumption? What did it take to do well as the listener?

What we often observe, ourselves, from this exercise is that the speaker is able to access thinking and feeling more easily, that they feel more deeply listened to and respected, and that the listener empathised with them. Does that last point surprise you? In spite of a lack of *explicit* empathy, the speaker feels strong empathy via the absence of advice and opinion.

Observation And Mindfulness

The Buddhist view of mindfulness provides some insights to the value of observational listening:

"Mindfulness (Sati) is mirror-thought. It reflects only what is presently happening and in exactly the way it is happening. There are no biases.
Mindfulness (Sati) is non-judgmental observation. It is that ability of the mind to observe without criticism. With this

ability, one sees things without condemnation or judgment. One is surprised by nothing. One simply takes a balanced interest in things exactly as they are in their natural states. One does not decide and does not judge. One just observes."
(Mindfulness in Plain English, Ven. Henepola Gunaratana)

> "Simply changing the way you listen to an observational style will improve your relationships and engagements with others by orders of magnitude."

Observation - of one's self, or of another, through listening - is a form of mindfulness. Through this, observational listening is one pathway to literally being in the Blue Zone. As you listen to observe, you allow judging, critical and advising thoughts to enter and leave, as would trains in a station, without racing to catch one. You have moved both your mind and response states from the narrow and the habitual (Red Zone), to having an almost unlimited number of potential objects of your attention.

In this state, you have most of your attention budget available and focused on the speaker. For the speaker, being listened to without judgement, advice or lots of interruption contributes powerfully towards moving them into their Blue Zone state. They feel included and respected. Through this mindful form of listening, they feel empathy from the listener, even where no empathy was literally or verbally expressed by the listener.

Now this is worth stopping to consider for a moment, for this is a key moment in this book. Simply changing the way you listen to an observational style will improve your relationships and engagements with others by orders of magnitude.

Andrew's journey of developing observational listening illustrates how you can move to this new listening state:

My inability to attend to myself or others through listening became most evident to me when I first tried to meditate. Back in 1995 I was in a heightened state of anxiety given the diagnosis of metastasised melanoma, and meditation seemed the best way to deal with the fear demons in my head. My mind at that point was so active, that I was unable to move into a more tranquil state: thoughts that came were hard to disengage with, and I would often find myself many minutes into a thought train 'journey'. My only saviour was the discovery of using evocative and gentle music to provide a point of focus and concentration. This allowed me to reach, with practice, some decent meditative states.

While this was working for me during my meditation sessions, its conscious impact in my day-to-day life was limited to allowing me to be in a calmer state. The impact on my relationships and engagements with other people was limited, and my listening, in particular, was no better. What

I see now is that my early attempts at meditation simply exposed the almost manic level of background activity in my mind. When I returned to the social world, this high level of activity was once again masked, and my listening was as it had always been: heavily distracted and diluted by my own thinking.

My next point of significant development came in 2004 when I did some coach training with David Rock. Very quickly I could see the degree to which my thinking was getting in the way of my listening. I was accessing assumptions, searching for answers, looking for ways to get the other person to see what I thought they needed, thinking about the shopping list… The wake up call came from my daughter, Stefanie. I had picked her up from school and she was telling me about her school day when she paused and said "Dad, you are not really listening, are you?" She was right - I had been caught thinking of three or four other things as she was speaking.

Since then, I have been paying much more attention, just to what I see and hear. No analysis, no assumption and advice only rarely. Trains of thought - something I have an impulse to say or ask - arrive and depart without me suddenly finding myself on them down the track. For me now, listening is tranquil and quiet, almost meditative, a strange irony given my early struggles with meditation itself.

Observational listening takes some effort in the first instance - your brain may well be comfortable with its habits of its own conversation as you listen. Focusing your attention and concentration on feeding back what you hear and see to the speaker is the first conscious step towards hard wiring this as a habit. Your first step towards deliberately using listening towards enhancing your influential leadership.

Active Listening vs Observational Listening

To many who have had experience, particularly in counseling, to *active listening*, there will be some close similarity between active and observational listening.

> "... we consume so much of our available brain bandwidth constructing what it is that we say, that we have little left to listen to what we actually say."

The most significant difference lies in the purpose of each: active listening has the explicit message of signaling to the speaker that you have, indeed, listened. While observational listening also achieves this, its primary purpose is to allow a person to hear what it is that they have said.

This feedback loop is critical for development - we consume so much of our available brain bandwidth constructing what it is that we say, that we have little left to listen to what we actually say. Observational listening is an amplification process, allowing a speaker to more strongly connect with their thinking and feeling, as expressed through their narrative.

Action Zone: Test And Practice Your Powers Of Observation

Identify a relationship (work, family or social) on which you would like to practice and develop your observational listening skills.

If you are not known as a good listener in the first instance, it may well be helpful to disclose to the other person what you are doing: the change can be startling, and we have had more than one female partner interrogate their husband/ boyfriend on what they are up to!

Observe, in the moment of conversation, anything you see and hear. Observe not only what is said, but what accompanies what is said. Look for things that you may not have seen or heard before.

When an opportunity arises, try feeding this back by starting with:
"What I hear is ..."
"What I see is ..."

Leave longer periods (than you might normally) where all you do is observe, not speak.

Limit your feedback to a *summary* of what you hear or see, and make sure that anything you give back is objective observation only.

Use the REACH conversation (see Chapter 10, Beyond Basic Conversations) as self-learning, or in a conversation with your partner to capture any learning and/or insight that arose from this exercise.

If you are a teacher - try this with one of your classes.
If you are a manager or leader, try this with one of your direct reports.
If you are a parent, try this with one of your teenage children.

Chapter 8

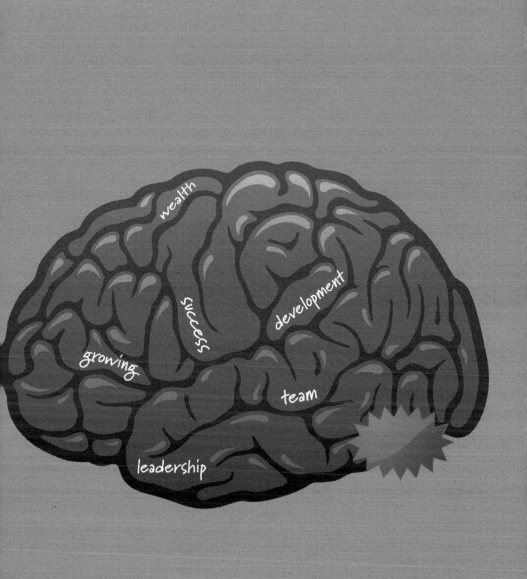

Optimistic Listening

"Few things in the world are more powerful than a positive push. A smile. A word of optimism and hope. And you can do it when things are tough."

Richard De Vos

Solution Responsibility

Whereas observational listening is re-tuning your attention away from you own cognition towards observing the conversation of another, optimistic listening is all about who has responsibility for finding the solution.

By default, we tend to take the position, or assumption, that we, the listener, are responsible for the solution to be found. To some degree this seems to be gender driven - John Gray, author of "Men are from Mars Women are from Venus", would suggest that male listeners like the point of the conversation to be clear, and that some sort of resolution is found. We would also suggest that the influence of 'management thinking' on leadership also drives towards the 'leader as listener' having the answer or solution. Both of these situations sees a dominant listening style of "Give me the details, so I can solve the problem for you".

This listening style remains appropriate and useful only when the outcome needed is informational: "Where is the stapler?", "How do I use Twitter for business", "What camera is best for wedding photography?" are examples.

Where at least one of the desired outcomes is growth in the capacity of a person in some way, listening to give the solution is a very *poor* growth tool.

Let's develop a scenario to test this: Sarah is a project manager, having responsibility for a team of twenty staff. Eric is project member, who is constantly missing key dates for project commitments. A number of projects have suffered delays because of Eric missing key commitments. Other project members are angry and anxious, but will challenge neither Sarah nor Eric on this situation.

When Sarah believes that it is her responsibility to solve Eric's time management, she will take the approach of asking questions that address the detail, problem and drama aspects of the situation. She will be listening to this information with the purpose of finding a solution herself, then giving this solution to Eric. She is listening with only part of her attention budget - a significant amount of her 'brain bandwidth' is being devoted to processing the detail and searching for a solution. Because of the need for efficiency (her resources are under strong demand), she will make assumptions about what Eric really needs. Eric, on the other hand, feels frustrated: he feels 'railroaded' into suggestions and advice that he instinctively knows is not the answer. He wants to improve, but is not motivated by Sarah's solutions. He feels both stuck, and down on himself for letting the team down.

This scenario is very much the default: for all of the right reasons, we often seek to find the answer for those we care for, or for whom we are responsible for in some way. What Sarah does not realise is that she is effectively sequestering a significant learning opportunity for both Eric and herself. Time to replay this scenario, using optimistic listening.

Sarah broaches the issue of missed commitments with Eric, firstly stating how things are as observations (not opinions, critiques or judgements). Using the best questions to help Eric access his thinking, she listens with the attitude and belief that Eric is responsible for finding a resolution to the issue. She helps him access potential answers by continuing to observe (as discussed in Chapter 7, Observational Listening). She may even, from time to time, offer helpful information, but because Eric has the mantle of responsibility for finding the solution, Sarah will allow Eric to decide what to do with this information. If his course of action is not ideal, the abstinence of Sarah from judging or correcting will allow Eric to take full learning advantage of any mistakes. This freedom to learn from error, of course, needs to be corralled by attention to personal and 'organisational' safety.

Because most of Sarah's brain bandwidth is available for listening to Eric, she is able to help him think his way towards a possible solution. She also learns a great deal more about Eric - his skills, attributes and challenges. Eric becomes energised by this conversation: his shortcomings have been acknowledged, but he has been given space and time to think, and a solution is emerging for him. Because it is his solution, it makes more logical and emotional sense to him, and he is far more committed to action. He feels listened to, respected and believed in, in spite of his past performance. He respects Sarah as a leader, and is beginning to feel like he wants to go out of his way not to let her down.

> Listening with the belief that the answer is within the speaker *will* leave the speaker feeling as if you *do* believe in them.

Optimistic listening is, then, an attitude and belief: unlike observational listening, it is not something you do, but more how you do it. In spite of this, it is no less detectable to the speaker. Listening with the belief that the answer is within the speaker *will* leave the speaker feeling as if you *do* believe in them.

To test the impact of where you believe the 'solution responsibility' to be, try this exercise.

Action Zone: Optimistic Listening Exercise

This exercise works best with a partner who is aware of what you are seeking to learn. Set this up so that your partner, who is the speaker, talks about a problem or issue that they would like to resolve. Give yourselves about ten minutes: the exercise is in two parts.

Part 1: The responsibility for the solution rests with the listener.

Begin conversing around the issue, with the listener adopting the deliberate attitude and belief that the *responsibility for finding the solution is with the listener.* "It is up to me as the listener to solve the problem." Time yourself with a device that will give you a signal five minutes in.

Part 2: The responsibility for the solution rests with the speaker.

When your timer signals you, make a strong and deliberate 180 degree shift in *where* the responsibility for the solutions sits: it is now up to the speaker to find the solution. It helps here if you adopt a strong expectation that the solution will emerge at any moment.

Insights and review:

Check in with the speaker about the key differences between the two halves of the exercise. What thinking and feelings arose out of each? What was the impact of each listening attitude?

When we run this exercise in large training groups, we often observe a significant drop in volume in the room between the first and second halves of this exercise. We realised one day that this is because one of the pairs - the listener - is talking much less. When we check in with the partner who was speaking, we found that they often felt 'conversationally crowded' - that there was no room for their own thinking. They felt frustrated and competitive - vying for the conversational space. Further, some speakers express frustration with solution-suggestions from their partner. This is commonly reported back to us as the least helpful part of the exercise.

We nearly always find a significant shift in the dynamic of the conversation when the listener shifts the seat of solution responsibility from themselves to the speaker. Now, the speaker experiences cognitive space, freedom to think, and again (as with observational listening) finds the feeling of respect and empathy from their partner. We also see a shift in the contribution from the listener: questions tend to replace statements. Many listeners, though not all, report that listening with this attitude takes some significant effort, such is the hard-wired habit of solution-finding for the other person when listening. They often find themselves wanting to offer advice or answers, and even still fall prey to indulging in providing the solution. In spite of this effort, a great unburdening is often reported by such people: they love the loss of solution responsibility as much as the gain in connection with the speaker.

Action Zone: Everyday Conversations

Develop your optimistic listening skills whenever you can by holding the expectation that the solution will emerge at any time from the other person. Use this in conjunction with your developing repertoire of powerful questions - these questions and optimistic listening naturally go hand in hand.

To begin, choose conversations where there is some element of the speaker needing to find their own growth, resolution or clarity. If someone wants to know where the order book is, and you know, holding the expectation that the answer will emerge from the other person will not work all that well for both of you! As you listen to any person that really does need to solve their own problem, focus on allowing them to own responsibility for their answer.

When you begin to feel comfortable with this strategic abandonment of having the solution yourself, combine this expectation that the answer will emerge with optimistic listening.

Conclusion

Listening has the potential to change the world. Period. The problem has been, until now, not understanding the attentional mechanism and purpose of how we listen. The concepts of optimistic and observational listening allow you to reshape your listening skills to better help another person grow. The good news is that this is a true win-win: as you provide the space for the capacity for the other person to grow, so too does reciprocal respect for you, not to mention your influence and charisma.

Optimistic and observational listening are universal habits of unconditional care and love: they apply to and enhance any relationship or engagement, whether you be leader, friend, partner, parent, lover, salesperson or teacher.

Chapter 9

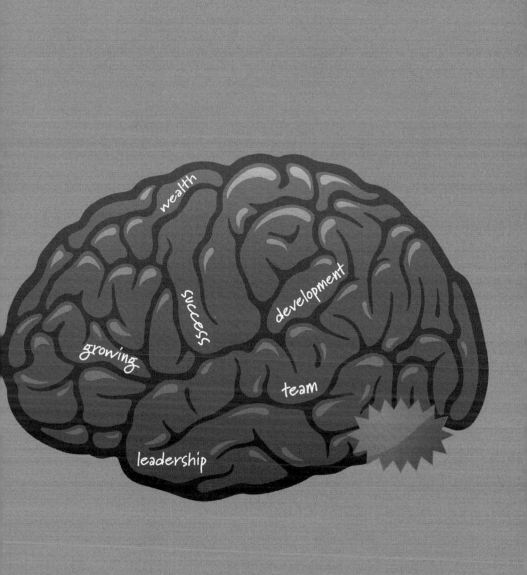

Conversations For Growth

"The basic building block of good communications is the feeling that every human being is unique and of value."

Unknown

The journey so far in this book has been to explore the mind state that underpins growth and adaptation, influence and unconditional respect: the Blue Zone. We have uncovered ways of managing down the Red Zone through a thinking approach to feelings and emotions. We have also looked at some communication mechanisms that align with Blue Zone engagements: using the best questions, and listening observationally and optimistically.

Now is the time to integrate all of this learning into a framework of conversations. This conversational framework will assist you to apply Blue Zone attitudes, behaviours and skills to a much greater and deeper degree.

The Four Conversations

Through our work with a number of creative, collaborative and generous people, we have identified four types of conversation:

Basic Conversations: the day-to-day conversations that take place within our relationships, our workplaces and within our own minds as self-talk.

Structured Conversations: usually framed on the basic conversation, but structured so as to achieve a specific purpose e.g. coaching, performance development, sales call, client engagements, etc.

Crucial Conversations: the conversations that need to take place, but that may be difficult either through elements of conflict, or deep-seated aversion to airing the issues.

Generative Conversations: the conversations that take place within a team that are creative and transformative i.e. that allows genuinely new solutions to emerge.

Worth emphasising, once more, is that for these conversations to reside truly in the Blue Zone, optimistic and observational listening have to be the default listening styles. True Blue Zone engagements also lack, in particular, judgement and assumption. Often, even when the best intentions are held for a conversation, the Red Zone intrudes in one way or another, leaving one or all in the conversation feeling frustrated, disappointed, or even angry.

In the remainder of this chapter we consider ways to apply the Blue Zone Habits of powerful questions and listening observationally and optimistically to Basic Conversations. In Chapter 10 we examine the more complex conversation types.

How What We Currently Do Gets In The Way

See if this conversation is familiar to you:

Sue (a team leader): "I am so struggling with all of this goal setting stuff - I feel so inadequate and such a fake ..."

Jack (her line manager): "You shouldn't feel like that - you got this job on your merits. You were the best for the job, you clearly beat the other three candidates."

Sue: "But look at Peta - she is just so organised, and I am so not ..."

Jack "Organisational ability was only one of the criteria. Look at how well you connect with the people in your team."

Sue: "Yes, I know, but what happens when I have to tell them what to do? What if they say no?"

Jack: "You'll be fine. You can always ask for help..."

Sue: "I know, but I'm sure others could be doing this better..."

Jack: "You have our confidence Sue, we believe in your ability. You just need to believe more in yourself."

Sue: "I know, I know - I just feel wrong in this position, I don't know why..."

This is a fairly common **basic** conversation: it is everyday in nature, it follows no formal set structure and it has emerged out of the general conversation or situation. While the content and context might change, the general feel and style would not be unfamiliar to you. Often, basic workplace conversations, like this one, address a multitude of people and process issues and problems.

One problem is, that without knowing it, we can be speaking to the wrong brain. In the conversation above, Sue is struggling to express herself with clarity because feelings and emotions are driving her narrative. She is speaking from her mammalian brain. Jack, however, is using rational, logical and evidentiary language to address her problem - he is speaking from his, and to her, rational brain - the neocortex. You will likely have had a number of these sorts of conversations - ones where you counter every rational objection, only for the other person to eventually say in frustration: "*I don't know, it's just not right...*". This is the point where the mammalian brain is no longer speaking 'through' the rational human brain, but speaking for itself.

Jonah Lehrer, in his recent book "The Decisive Moment", says:

"One of the enduring paradoxes of the human mind is that it doesn't know itself very well. The conscious brain is ignorant

of its own underpinnings and is blind to all that neural activity taking place outside the prefrontal cortex. This is why people have emotions: they are windows into the unconscious, visceral representations of all the information we process but don't perceive." (P236, The Decisive Moment)

It is, as he puts it, that we know more than we know. The narrative we tend to use, by default, is very good at addressing the rational brain, but very poor at interpreting the emotional brain. This makes sense: the language centre is well entrenched in the cortex, allowing the human brain to speak well for itself. Not so the mammalian/emotional brain - it must recruit the cortex to speak on its behalf. Yet the mammalian brain, as relatively inaccessible as it is, houses learning from experience. In so doing, it has access to the circuitry of both wisdom and folly.

While Jack's purpose above is noble, the impact of this conversation on Sue does not match his intent. Through this default conversation, he has not been able to assist Sue to move forward in any way. He may have even entrenched the blocks that help her stay stuck.

Before we return to Sue and Jack's conversation, it might be helpful to consider a model from "The Seven Cs of Coaching" by Mick Cope. In helping coaches understand the person and their picture, Cope describes the "3D me" model, where the three dimensions or 'influencers' are Head, Heart and Hand.

Head: what people are thinking or saying (to themselves or others)

Heart: feelings and emotions that are impacting

Hand: factors arising from behaviours and actions

This model shows the collision of Jack and Sue's conversation: Jack is addressing Sue's Head, while she is expressing an issue arising from her Heart. As Cope puts it:

"The aim for pulling together these three diverse groups of ideas is to help develop a more cohesive and congruent coaching framework - one that takes into account the whole person and not just particular emotional, logical or behavioural factors." (P37, The Seven Cs of Coaching).

Translating this coaching context into having better basic conversations, we would do better if we took into account all three dimensions that might be influencing the other person. What Sue is feeling is: inadequacy, fear of letting others down, illegitimacy in her role.

How To Improve Your Basic Conversations

Given that basic conversations are ad hoc and not necessarily intentional or structured, planning what to say in such situations is not very useful. Having the best basic conversations is all about putting together understanding of the Blue and Red Zones, knowing the most engaging way to listen and using dialogue that is most helpful.

Be aware of your Red and Blue Zone states

By definition, if you are aware to some degree of your emotional and thinking states, then equally to some degree, you are in a Blue Zone mind state. Having and using this awareness while you engage with others is a key point of this book: this awareness allows you to better self manage. In the moment of the conversation, for example, you might become aware of an intrusion of an unhelpful thought or feeling. Your awareness notes the intrusion, like a train arriving at a station. This awareness also allows this train of thought or feeling to depart without you on it, an act of self-management. The space that you create by not engaging with yourself in this way allows thinking to flow for the other person.

Listen more than you speak

As discussed extensively in the listening chapters, how, and to what you listen are critical elements in getting the best out of any conversation. Optimistic and observational listening both allow a person to experience reflection, clarity and even insight. Just as the moon moves in front of the sun, listening to solve someone's issue for them will eclipse their own clarity.

Problems or issues may, or may not arise in basic conversations. Our model of optimistic listening, believing that the solution will emerge *from* them at any time, may not seem to always fit here. Yet holding a strong position of unconditionality - for them and their current reality - is a critical underpinning of listening well in basic conversations. Abandonment of assumption and judgement are goals for you here - allow judging or predictive thoughts to come and go without connecting with them.

For Jack in our earlier conversation, it may have been better for him to spend less of his attention budget on reassuring Sue, and more on listening from an observational purpose.

Observe and ask more than you tell

Observational listening, when employed in basic conversations, provides excellent conversational fodder: giving succinct and objective observation back to a speaker is fuel for their own thinking. Indeed, this helps maintain the reflection-clarity-insight cycle that leads to a self-discovered solution. Jack may have been better to observe and feed back to Sue something like:

"I can see the emotion..." or "So you feel that you are struggling in the role⋯"

Questions are also a critical element of effective basic conversation and are particularly powerful when combined with an observation. The best questions to use in basic conversations are simple, yet open-ended. To help Sue in her dilemma, Jack could have said:

"I can see the emotion··· how would you like to feel?" or "So you feel that you are struggling in the role··· how would you like to feel?"

A good rule of thumb is to ask or observe more than you tell. In ad-hoc conversations, anywhere from 50-50 to 70-30 of listening to speaking seems to be a good mix. Mentoring might be one exception to this ratio: where you have some key experience or content to provide, the balance might temporarily shift back towards more speaking than listening.

If you have to 'Tell', follow immediately with 'Ask'

Sometimes you need to give some information, be it advice, a hint or clue towards a possible solution, or perhaps an observation that is 'telling it how it is'. One secret of the charismatic and influential is the tell-ask skill: whenever you need to 'tell', always follow with 'ask'. For Sue's situation, Peter could say:

"From my point of view we actually value your people skills more than your need to develop time management. What thinking emerges for you, knowing that?"

Most often, the sort of question that works best is one that directs the attention of the speaker in some way to their *thinking*.

This works very well whenever you need to give some information, advice for example, that you need the speaker to process and integrate in some way.

Use questions that focus on the present or future more than the past

As you would have seen in Chapter 5, questions have the potential to lift a conversation into the realm of possibilities, or sink into the mire of detail, problem and drama. Having a repertoire of questions that lead to reflection, clarity and insight is a critical element of engaging in positive basic conversations.

Acknowledgement

Many of us are uncomfortable with overt displays of emotion in social situations. Uncertainty seems to trigger off some level of social anxiety. When someone tearfully says *"It's all too much for me, I can't get through this, I just can't see it happening…"* a very common response is "I understand how you feel…". While the intent is empathy, the impact often falls short. The speaker will have a good chance of thinking *"How could you understand???"*, for this might be the cumulative statement of a whole range of issues, some of which you know nothing about. Noteworthy is that the response is still an 'I' statement - something about me, the listener.

A much more enabling (for the speaker) response is to simply acknowledge what you see or hear (observation again): "I can see the emotion there⋯", or "So you feel stuck?" This shows the speaker that you are listening, feeds back critical clarifying information and does not transmit opinion, judgement or advice.

Did you notice that you can acknowledge through a question? This is particularly powerful, even necessary, when you are synthesising a 'theme' to feed back to the speaker. The words "So you feel stuck⋯?", above were not the words of the speaker, but seem to be what is being said. Putting this back to the speaker as a question allows them to confirm or reject the query, and, in either case, the outcome is clarity for the speaker.

Returning to Sue and Jack's conversation, this might look like:

Sue: "I am so struggling with all of this goal setting stuff - I feel so inadequate and such a fake ..."

Jack: "I can see your frustration - is this about confidence for you?"

Rather than being told how she should feel ("You shouldn't feel like that - you got this job on your merits), she can now access her thinking at a conceptual (not detail) level and respond:

"You're right, it is about confidence···", or

"Hmmm··· I'm not so sure it's confidence - it's more about organisation ···"

In either case, the acknowledgement and observation-as-question provides access to a greater understanding of her situation and she is the one making the call.

Permission

Uncertainty and lack of perceived autonomy or control are two significant Red Zone triggers. Where acknowledgement largely addresses uncertainty, permission reduces Red Zone activation by providing clarity and perceived autonomy. In coaching, permission is effectively used when a coach detects Red Zone energy - usually anxiety of some sort - in either the coach or coachee. Often it is a signal you are moving onto 'shaky' conversational ground and a simple "Are you OK for me to ask about this?" provides control to the coachee, and clarity on progression of the conversation.

> "...permission reduces Red Zone activation by providing clarity *and* perceived autonomy."

In our training, we demonstrate the effectiveness of permission by asking participants to consider asking us two questions: one question that would be easy to ask (about anything) and a second question that they would find very difficult to ask, in a social context - safe and outrageous, in other words. While there are a few outcomes of this exercise, it becomes obvious that asking "Do you mind if I ask you a difficult question?" in front of the outrageous question removes most of the sting of the latter.

In basic conversations, you might use permission to create the space for a Crucial Conversation:

"David, I need to have a crucial conversation with you - when would be best today to do that?"

In general terms, permission is very powerful for managing down any potential intrusion of the Red Zone, yet it is also very much under-utilized in basic conversations.

Silence in Basic Conversations

Silence often leaves people feeling uncomfortable - the uncertainty that accompanies silence can trigger social anxiety and subsequently the Red Zone. Many people will prefer to fill silent moments, even with meaningless chatter in some cases, over allowing the silence to feed any anxiety. Silence, however, can be a powerful, if underutilized, conversational tool: it can allow for, and create the space (and sometimes the pressure) for innovative and insightful thinking to emerge.

The following are indications that silence might move the conversation forward:

- If you find yourself interrupting by talking over someone else
- Thinking of what you're going to say when someone is talking
- 'Knee-jerk' reactions where you respond without thinking first
- When you find yourself 'demonstrating your expertise' because you feel insecure
- Offering advice before the other person has had a chance to fully explain the situation
- When you're doing most of the talking
- When you create a distraction by changing topics
- Saying the same thing over and over again

(*From Fierce Conversations: Achieving Success at Work* by Susan Scott)

Applying Basic Conversation Principles

Let's now return to Sue and Jack's conversation and see if we can merge Jack's intent with his impact, using the concepts outlined so far.

Sue: "I am just so struggling with all of this goal setting stuff - I feel so inadequate and such a fake ..."

Jack: "Is that something that you want to chat about now?" [Permission]

Sue: "Yeah - I guess. It's been on my mind...

Jack "I can hear your frustration - would this be about confidence?" [Acknowledgement]

Sue: "It is, and it isn't. I look at the others who might have got the job, and I see so much capability"

Jack: "What might you need so that you feel more confident?"

Sue: "If I could be more organised, I'd feel like I at least had all of the tasks in control..."

Jack: "How might that look for you?"

Sue: "I'm not sure, organisation is not my forte, but I know that I need to get on top of it. I know I'm good with getting the best out of others, I'm just not so good at applying that to myself..."

From here, the conversation might go in a number of directions. Jack may just listen more, letting Sue speak, or if needed, he might ask permission around whether Sue might like to have a Structured Conversation, such as coaching, to help her move forward. The thing is, she has not been *told* how to feel, nor has she necessarily been told what to do. Jack has conveyed belief in her, empathy and respect. Sue feels far more enabled and far less frustrated than she might have at the start of the conversation. She also now has a clearer path towards building her own capacity.

Basic Conversations: Moving People from Red to Blue

Throughout this book we have been positioning the maladaption of the Red Zone in solving social and emotional issues. We have also been holding up the Blue Zone as a mind state where these same issues can be resolved, both within or between people. Through emotional contagion, we know that the emotional state, and hence either the Red or Blue Zone state, of another person is catching. This is the neurological mechanism that underpins both road rage at one end of the scale, and social inclusion and affiliation at the other. Street riots versus Luther King's "I have a dream" speech.

In our day-to-day living, we often come up against Red Zones - those that belong to us, or that belong to others around us. While, as we discussed in Chapter 4 (A Brain For The 21st Century), we can work on our own emotional state by thinking our way to being calm under pressure, it is through conversation that we can have that same impact on another person. Take the following example:

Angry Parent: "I am so tired of my son being picked on. This is bullying - what are you going to do about it??? I want that bully to be suspended!"

Principal: "Mandy, I have said to you before that we have a procedure and a policy here. I will decide what to do about the situation - I refuse to allow you to dictate my actions here!"

We have often found ourselves in adversarial conversations, where each party's Red Zone infects and escalates that of the other. Peter, the principal in the above exchange, may well be right. Yet *countering* the other party has a history littered with failure. Using the elements of successful basic conversations outlined in this chapter, Peter can bring Mandy more into the Blue Zone, and through this pathway, also bring himself back into his success zone:

Mandy: "I am so tired of my son being picked on. This is bullying - what are you going to do about it??? I want that bully to be suspended!"

Peter: "Thanks for bringing my attention to this - I can see your anger and frustration Mandy. I'm very keen to have this resolved - would you prefer to sit with me over a cup of tea or perhaps go for a walk while we talk this out?"

In spite of Peter, himself, starting in the Red Zone with Mandy's aggressive concern over her son's bullying, taking a position of listening optimistically and observationally, and through using helpful questions and dialogue Peter can transport both Mandy and himself into a 'zone of resolution'.

Action Zone: Enhancing Basic Conversations

The next time you find yourself in dispute with your partner at home, particularly where you recognise perhaps a little late that both of you are in your Red Zones, try taking a strong stance using observation, acknowledgement and helpful questions. Questions like:

If this were to be resolved, what would be different for you?

What assumptions are we making here?

How could I contribute to a resolution?

How could you contribute to a resolution?

What should we do next?

But What If I Am Paid To Have The Answer?

By now, you will have seen a strong theme of not telling another person how it is that they should feel, or what it is that they should do. Those of you reading this from a leadership context might have some challenges arising out of this theme: "My direct reports expect answers from me" or "It is my job, at least sometimes, to tell people what to do" are common responses at this stage.

To clarify this, where learning and growth are not primary outcomes, and where clarity, capacity and purpose exist, then telling someone what it is they need to do is consistent with everything in this book. In this context, "I need you to⋯" works perfectly well. Where a person lacks clarity, lacks understanding of the purpose or lacks capability in some way, then they need to undertake an *internal* learning journey to be able to meet the demand. This latter context is where we can be far more effective by having conversations that are defined by the Blue Zone elements of listening, questioning, acknowledgement and permission. It is through these elements that we create the conditions for a person to access their own learning.

Providing leadership clarity to your direct reports is also critical here. When a direct report needs growth in their own capacity in some way, it is very helpful, if not essential, to let them know that your role is to help them think better about the situation, not necessarily to find the answer for them. This does not preclude you from providing them with information, clues towards, or examples of possible solutions. In the end, it is what sense they make of this information and how well you help them access this sense, through their own thinking, that is important. The best leaders do this, as do the best teachers and the best parents.

In conclusion here, let's return to a point we made in Chapter 3, (Your Mind Zones In Action). We said that our research shows that what students need, aside from safety and professional teaching skills are: teachers that unconditionally respect, listen, and believe in the potential of students. We also made the point that these needs are not restricted to only students - these are the basic and universal requirements of thriving, regardless of context or organisation.

How are these needs met, then, in basic (or indeed, any of the other) conversations?

In chapter 5, we spoke of powerful questioning, a dialogue that is much more useful and developmental than giving solutions, advice or opinion. It turns out that when the coach/leader uses questions and language that lack advice, answers or opinion, the speaker makes the very strong inference that they have not been judged, that they have been unconditionally accepted. This maps potently to a feeling of unconditional respect. Hence, our model of powerful questioning addresses the provision of respect.

During the moment of observational listening, a speaker experiences a clear sense of having been heard. The absence of adversarial listening - listening to have my say - gives an unassailable knowledge of having been listened to.

Optimistic listening, listening with the belief that the answer will emerge from the speaker, is clearly detectable by the speaker. It runs parallel with students detecting a belief in their ability from an outstanding teacher. These underpinning attitudes supply a powerful and enabling social connection between speaker and listener.

> "The absence of adversarial listening – listening to have my say - gives an unassailable knowledge of having been listened to."

Without doubt then, adopting these communication attitudes and behaviours significantly impact on the core necessities of thriving relationships:

Powerful Questioning = Unconditional Respect
Observational Listening = Being Listened To
Optimistic Listening = Being Believed In

These skills of engagement are deeply seated in Blue Zone brain regions and if used to underpin any of the four conversations, will create huge opportunities for growth for both speaker and listener.

Action Zone: Drawing It All Together

Over the period of a week, choose three workplace conversations, with peers or people whom you lead, and apply your learning in a focused and deliberate way. Take the time to pull together your developing skills of using helpful dialogue (questions for growth) and observational/ optimistic listening.

For greater rigour in testing the effect of these conversations, prepare these peers or direct reports by asking them to rate your current conversations in terms of how helpful they are, how much clarity you add, how well you listen and the degree to which these people feel that you help them grow. Ask them to re-rate after your 'practice' conversation.

Chapter 10

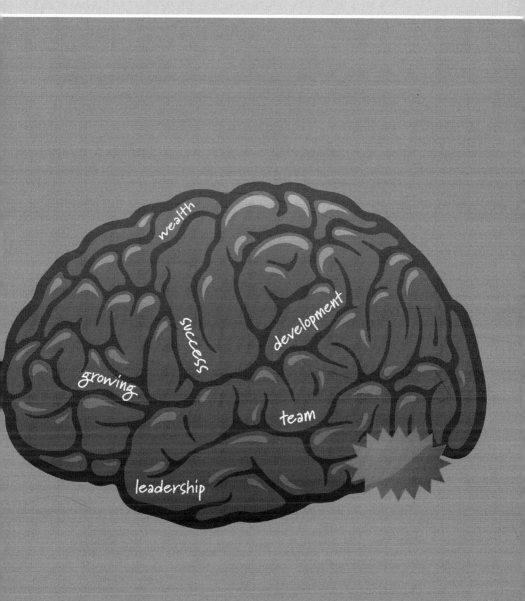

Beyond Basic Conversations

"Speak as though you're certain, listen as though you're not."

Richard Olivier (son of Sir Lawrence)

This chapter will extend your awareness and skill-set around Blue Zone Habits and Basic Conversations into conversation types that have higher stakes and enhanced outcomes.

Structured Conversations

Structured conversations, guided by frameworks and protocols, are most often used in the workplace and rarely in personal relationships.

Each conversation, as such, has a desired outcome or purpose, and usually has a form of progression that assists movement towards that outcome. Examples of structured conversations include:

- Formal coaching conversations
- Workplace review and appraisal
- Formal meetings
- Relationship counselling
- Job interviews
- Court proceedings

In the context of this book, the explicit purpose and outcome for a structured conversation is growth: growth in capacity, quality of relationship, delivery of service or even quality of life. Just as in Basic Conversations, key elements · of listening, acknowledging, gaining permission and using thinking questions should be present if a structured conversation is to provide real opportunities for growth and learning.

The conversations we will suggest here have their roots in coaching, and have the outcomes of making sense of something ("What does this mean to me?") and taking action ("What I might do?"). Indeed, an adaptation of the existential cycle for change shows how these two questions are an integral part of this process:

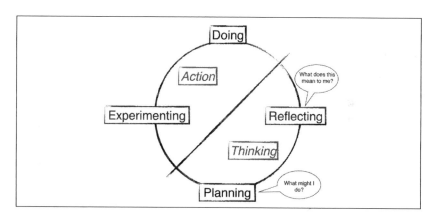

As the above diagram shows, a new 'doing' is not possible without reflection, planning and experimentation. We are going to suggest two core, structured conversations, each addressing reflecting and planning. Most other structured conversations will flow as variations to these two core forms. In each case, you will find a characteristic that, for us, separates coaching conversations from most others: a drive to action. Action forms the content for the next phase of reflection and planning. Action and thinking are very much yin and yang, and should lead natively from one to the other, for learning to be continuous.

Maintaining Clarity In Structured Conversations

A point of difference between structured and basic conversations is the need to have greater clarity around the roles within structured conversations. Given that two key Red Zone triggers are ambiguity and lack of perceived autonomy, it is most helpful if the speaker or coachee is aware of the purpose, outcomes and the 'hats to be worn'. Structured conversations for growth should foster reflection, clarity and insight, in that order. If a coachee begins to wonder "Why isn't she giving me the solution?" or "Is he asking this as a coach, or as my manager", then they have moved out of reflection and will not achieve clarity or insight.

We would suggest a small 'spiel' before beginning any structured conversation, one that clears the space for the coachee. When we begin to coach, we usually say something along the lines of:

"This is a coaching conversation. I am going to assist you to reflect on some feedback towards determining a professional goal that will interest and challenge you.

I'm not in the role of providing answers or solutions, but simply to assist you to think more clearly around all the things that could be considered.

You might find me asking the same question, looking for more than a single response from that question. This is not because I haven't found an answer I am looking for, just a part of the process of looking under a number or stones, so to speak.

I will also be holding you to consider things from a vision and planning perspective - if we get bogged down in detail then it is likely that you will not gain as much clarity or insight. Is it OK if I interrupt you if we do get bogged down in detail?

Do you have any questions about what we are going to do?"

The whole point here is to, as best we can, anticipate any unknowns the coachee might have, particularly if they have not experienced a coaching conversation before. Note the reference to detail above - as the coach I am not only laying out how I will conduct myself, but how it is that I need the coachee to think. This also gives us the license to bring the coachee back up to a level of thinking where they can make connections in their thinking.

This clearing the space for the conversation becomes critical when the coach is also a middle manager, or has some role other than coaching within the organisation. It is a symbolic, deliberate 'swapping of the hats' from one role to the other, that provides the conversation clarity. It goes without saying that the coach needs to stay true to the role: if there is a strong and pressing and immediate need to cover something outside of the structured conversation, then we would suggest being clear about suspending the conversational role:

"I am just going to step out of coaching for the moment, so that I can cover this as your line manager - is that OK?"

While this should be a rarity, it helps maintain integrity and trust in the process of the structured conversation.

Help Another Reflect Through DREAM

DREAM is a particular conversation framework that we use in our own coaching. This structured conversation creates the conditions to effectively reflect on the meaning of an input; whether this be around feedback, in exploring clarity on an issue or problem, or towards determining an interesting and challenging goal. The skeleton of this conversation is DREAM:

Define the issue
Present Reality around the issue
Envision the future ideal state
Alternative courses of action towards the desired future
Make it happen: what action will you take now that you know this.

As with all conversations for growth, it is critical that the listener attend with observational and optimistic purpose.

Questions That Fit DREAM

We have some examples of DREAM conversational guides that can be downloaded from:
http://www.thesuccesszone.com/resources.

We also have some video and audio examples of how these guides might be used. Alternatively, asking a series of questions that best fit the current position of the DREAM process from the list below, as a more 'casual' approach might also be a way to conduct a DREAM conversation.

Define the Issue:

What do you really want to explore today?

What is the change you wish to make?

What triggered the desire to take action?

What will be the benefit for you in making the change? For others?

How is this issue/change important to you?

What will success look like here?

How long do you want this change to last for?

How will you know that you have achieved this?

How will things be different, once you have made this change?

Can you bring that down to one sentence? How about 5-10 words?

What is the present <u>Reality</u>?

How do you see the current situation?

Would you say that you are in a Blue or Red Zone state on this issue?

On a scale of 1 to 10, how far into the Blue Zone are you? (10 is completely Blue)

On a scale of 1 to 10, how much is the Red Zone intruding? (10 is completely intruding)

On a scale of 1 to 10, how anxious are you feeling on this issue?

How would you rate your current level of performance/ satisfaction/effectiveness*, say out of 10? (*adapt this to the context as needed)

How long have you been thinking about this?

How often do you think about it?

What are the two or three key emotions that you feel around this issue?

How would someone else describe this situation? (e.g. peers, friends, family)

What do you feel when you think about this issue?

What is the evidence for how you think or feel about the issue?

What evidence might you be missing? What evidence counters your thinking?

What thoughts or self-talk do you notice when you are in this situation?

How does this issue impact on how you are with others? How does this issue affect others?

How is your thinking or feeling impacting on how you act/behave?

Is this issue in your top 3, top 5 or top 10 issues?

How is this issue/change important to you?

What things or values would you never give up on?

What is within my control to change?

Envision the future state

What are the criteria for a perfect solution?

If things were perfect tomorrow, what would you see that is different to today?

If things were perfect tomorrow, what would you feel that is different to today?

What rating on the Blue Zone scale (out of 10) would you like to be experiencing?

How would you rate your ideal level of performance/ satisfaction/effectiveness*, say out of 10?

(*adapt this to the context as needed)

Imagine that you are now at your desired rating. What do you see and feel that is different to today?

How would you like to feel/think/act in this situation?

What two or three emotions would you like to feel, in a perfect state?

If there were no limitations, what would be the ideal situation here?

How strong, say out of 10, would you say your hunger or desire for a solution is?

How would you like to be thinking in an ideal version of this situation?

How would you like to be feeling in an ideal version of this situation?

How do you need to be thinking for an ideal outcome here?

How do you need to be feeling for an ideal outcome here?

Alternative courses of action

Imagine you have reached your goal, and we are talking about having reached it now. Looking back, what steps did you take to get here?

What would the person you most admire do in this situation?

What thinking/feeling/acting would most help you move towards your goal here?

What would me the most conservative alternative?

What would be the most outrageous alternative?

What alternatives lie in between?

What assumptions are you making in thinking about alternatives?

What alternatives arise if you remove these assumptions? What information might lead you to finding more alternatives?

What alternatives would you never consider? What stops you from considering them?

*Making it **H**appen*

How clear about your next steps are you?

What do you need for more clarity on your next steps?

What barriers might you anticipate?

Is there anything you need to abandon to me able to take action from here?

What steps will you take now?

When will these steps happen?

What assistance might you need to complete these steps?

Goal Strength

A coachee should have a strong sense of clarity on an emergent goal, or goals. It is worth checking on goal strength at this stage, this being a measure of its 'stickiness'. A 'sticky' goal is likely to stay 'front of mind', and is much more likely to impact on the growth of a coachee.

Is it a stretch? Learning emerges from stretch and discomfort. Without stretch, a person stays in their status quo.

Is it achievable? A goal beyond realistic attainment is a goal that will not be subconsciously considered.

If it is emotive: without strong connection and 'approval' by the mammalian brain, there is little to motivate.

Integrate Insight: REACH

The REACH conversation framework is the natural follow-up to the DREAM conversation. It fits where the question "What does this mean to me, my goal or my growth" needs to be answered.

It is a perfect framework for assessing the learning or impact from feedback or action, learning from observing another person in action, or from information that does not fit the 'current world' of a person. It can also be adapted to fit performance review processes, or any situation where new action arising from learning is a desired outcome.

Once the DREAM conversation has established the goal or focus, the REACH conversation can be repeated cyclically, given that it finishes with "What will I do now that I know this?" (H, what Happens next), which elegantly creates the starting point (R, current Reality) for the next iteration of this conversation.

Through this mechanism, attention can be paid strategically to creating new brain wiring by addressing the two states, action and thinking about action, needed to create a newly learned habit. In adults, new *permanent* habits take about two to three months of repetitive attention to 'hard wire'. Bringing deliberate attention to this learning cycle once or twice a fortnight seems to be sufficient for the brain to cement its adaptation.

Again, the person managing the conversation, the coach for want of a better word, needs to pay attention to creating the best conditions for the speaker or coachee to reflect and find clarity and insight. The REACH framework is a somewhat 'tighter' conversation than DREAM in spite of its flexibility:

Present Reality around the action taken, feedback or information given

Emotions that accompany the action taken, feedback or information given

Acquire - what did you gain or learn from the action taken, feedback or information given

Connections - what connections or implications arise from action taken, feedback or information given

Happens Next? - New action that arises out of the learning and connections made.

Questions That Fit The REACH Framework

A guide outlining the REACH conversation can be found at http://www.thesuccesszone.com/resources. For a more 'casual' approach to asking questions around this framework, the following questions will be of some use:

Present Reality

How did [the action] go for you? What did you notice or see as a result?

How would you rate the effectiveness of your action, say out of 10? (Relate back to desired rating)

What happened for you?

What stands out in the feedback for you?

What do you find challenging or unexpected in the feedback?

What did you find challenging or unexpected in completing the action (or observing the action in peer observation)?

How has this action/feedback/observation moved you towards your goal?

Emotions

What emotions did you notice in completing the action(s) (or in observing your peer)?

What emotions arose in viewing/hearing your feedback?

What emotion stands out for you?

Are there any unexpected or challenging emotions for you in this?

What Red Zone emotions or anxieties arose for you?

What Blue zone feelings arose for you?

Acquire

What have you learnt from doing this?

What have you gained from your actions (or from observing your peer)?

Has the feedback provided you with any insights or learning?

Is there something that you now know, that was not obvious to you before?

Connections

Are there any new connections happening in your thinking that result from your learning?

What are the implications for what you have learnt?

What possibilities arise for you from what you have learnt?

Is there anything that seems to be missing arising from your learning?

Is there anything that you know that you don't know now, as a result of your learning?

What do you need to explore now that you know this?

Happens Next?

What actions arise out of this conversation?

What could or will you do now that you know this?

What actions could continue your learning here?

Are there any conversations that you now need to have as a result of your learning?

Adapting The REACH Conversation

The REACH conversation can be adapted to almost any situation where the learning from action, behaviour or information is a desired outcome. It can be used as a single 'intervention' to build awareness, or as a repetitive cycle to extend the capacity of a person permanently in some way. In each of these different variations of REACH, all that need change is the input into the process, whether this be something that the person has tried, an undesirable behaviour, formal or informal feedback or something that the person has strategically or casually observed as professional practice.

Some of the ways we have seen REACH used include:

Managing performance targets for direct reports

Building student awareness around the impact of their behaviour

Building emotional resilience

Creating a learning culture from peer observation

Getting the most out of 360 degree feedback

Examples of these different adaptations of REACH can be downloaded at http://www.thesuccesszone.com/resources.

Action Zone: Use REACH

Use the REACH conversation as a mechanism to further develop one of the methods of staying cool under pressure (Chapter 4). Choose one of the four methods you would like to be better at, and commit to some actions to build this capacity. Use the REACH framework to self coach around your learning and next steps.

Download the DREAM and REACH conversation guides from http://www.thesuccesszone.com/resources and practice these conversations with a peer or willing direct report.

Feedback your growth and insights from leading these conversations at http://www.thesuccesszone.com/forums and interact with others moving through their own coaching journey.

Crucial Conversations

In their work on Crucial Conversations, Kerry Patterson, Joseph Grenny, Ron McMillan and Al Switzler would define such conversations as those "between two or more people where stakes are high, opinions vary and emotions run strong". Given the high stakes, the mammalian brain's loss aversion is likely to be, at least, partly to blame for seeking to avoid such conversations. Other factors, such as our brain's preference for comfort and efficiency, a socially hard-wired distaste for conflict and simply not knowing what to say, contribute to some conversations being swept under the carpet.

> "Critical to the success of such a conversation; planned or otherwise, is *knowing* that you are, indeed, in a crucial conversation. This awareness then allows you to pay extra attention to creating the necessary conditions for success."

In our recent conversations with leaders, it seems that an emerging insight is that organisations are developing conversational mechanisms for increasing the potential for vertical crucial conversations, yet the horizontal crucial conversations are often simply not happening. In other words, 'speaking up' (and down) with difficult conversations has been enabled, yet creating the capacity for peers to have such conversations with each other has not.

In our view, Crucial Conversations could take the form of either a Basic or a Structured Conversation. While most will occur between two people as a one-on-one engagement, this type of conversation may also take the form of one-to-many, many-to-one and many-to-many. People may find that they are, all of a sudden, in the middle of a crucial conversation, or they may well have been able to anticipate and plan such an engagement.

Critical to the success of such a conversation; planned or otherwise, is *knowing* that you are, indeed, in a crucial conversation. This awareness then allows you to pay extra attention to creating the necessary conditions for success.

Spontaneous Crucial Conversations

When you find yourself, often with a sudden realisation, in the middle of a conversation where opinions, emotions and the risks are significant, it is critical that this new awareness shapes and sharpens your attention. The guidelines for successful Basic Conversations apply here:

Be aware of your Red and Blue Zone states

Listen more than you speak, using optimistic and observational listening

Ask more than you tell

Follow tell, with ask

Use questions that focus on the present and future more than the past

Use Acknowledgement and Permission

Allow for silence to sit and generate.

It is likely, given the nature of these conversations, that Red Zones from either party will begin to intrude, so paying particular attention to staying calm under pressure is a prerequisite for success here too. Awareness within the mammalian brain of the potential social risk will activate the reptilian brain's survival architecture.

Planned Crucial Conversations

On some occasions, you will have the luxury of anticipating and even planning for a crucial conversation. The preparation that you put into this conversation will strongly determine the degree of its success: anticipated crucial conversations that lack preparation often descend into difficult and painful Red Zone engagements. Aspects to pay attention to in readying for a planned crucial conversation should include:

Timing, Environment: when and where would be best to conduct the conversation? Often neutral and novel (i.e. new) locations assist in conversational success, particularly if there is a history of previous difficult engagements. Giving a decent amount of time, removing as many external 'deadline' pressures as possible, also contributes to a successful outcome.

Pre-conversation reflection: using a set of questions, the leader of the conversation, or even in some cases, all participants, may benefit from preparing their thinking though reflection. Questions that could trigger useful reflection include:

What is preventing you from having this conversation?

What are the risks in not having this conversation?

What key emotions are present as you think about this conversation and its context?

What has to shift for you to approach this conversation with generosity?

What assumptions are you making about yourself and/or the other person?

If you were in the other person's shoes, how would you see this situation?

What would you like the outcome or resolution to be?

If this situation were resolved, what would be different?

Define the conversation, issue: use questions (from DREAM for instance) that assist in objectively outlining and defining the issue. Create the conversational space by also attending to the way people engage (optimistic, objective, respectful)

Explore the impact: use present reality questions that explore the impact of the current situation, allowing for acknowledgement of emotions and thoughts.

Agree on a Shared Future: use questions that explore desired future states, possible options and agreed actions.

Check for Understanding: use questions that determine that parties to the conversation 'are on the same page'.

Noteworthy is the use of silence, as discussed in improving basic conversations in (Chapter 9) – it can be a powerful enabler of the solution in a Planned Crucial Conversation.

Examples of Structured Crucial Conversation guides can be downloaded from http://www.thesuccesszone.com/resources.

Generative Conversations

Generative Conversations occur usually in teams, though sometimes between two people, that are creative, collaborative and transformative. These are the conversations that invent and re-invent an organisation, that allow an organisation to adapt and learn. Because these conversations generate brand-new thinking and solutions, they are genuine and complete Blue Zone conversations. Any intrusion of a participant's Red Zone has the potential to derail these engagements: generative conversations, then, are enabled though pre-requisite Crucial Conversations that 'clear the air'.

With participants in these conversations needing to be strongly in their own Blue Zone, leaders (of the conversation and the organisation) need to attend to creating the necessary conditions:

Mutual and unconditional respect between and amongst participants

A known and experienced shared vision for the group and/or organisation

Diversity and ambiguity are permissioned and held as important 'ingredients'

There is a culture of listening and believing in members of the conversation and organisation

What should be emerging here, is that the ability for a team to have a generative conversation is a reflection of the culture of the organisation. Without the organisation making evolutionary, sometimes revolutionary steps towards being a Blue Zone organisation, true Generative Conversations will remain beyond it's reach.

Chapter 11

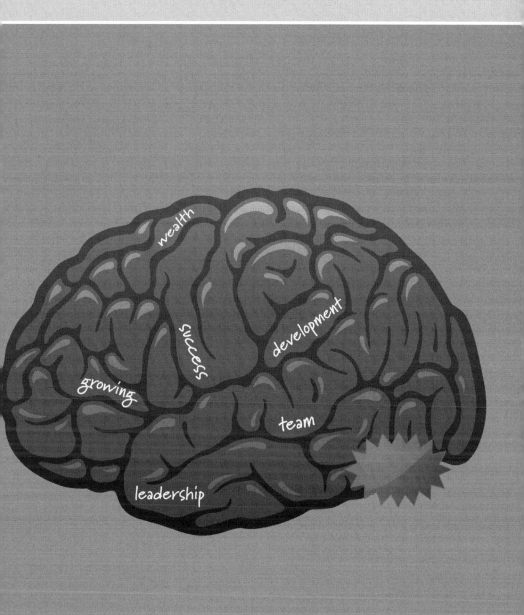

Leadership For A New World

"We can't solve problems by using the same kind of thinking we used when we created them."
Albert Einstein

"So, first of all, let me assert my firm belief that the only thing we have to fear is fear itself - nameless, unreasoning, unjustified terror which paralyzes needed efforts to convert retreat into advance."
Franklin D Roosevelt 1933

A Red Zone World

Gary is a middle-level manager in a medium-sized organisation. As he drives to work, he experiences anger, anxiety and selfishness from drivers around him. On the radio, he hears of another rape, another act of terrorism, another youth suicide, more sub-prime fuelled economic news. His own children seem distant and alien to him, and he worries about the world that they are inheriting.

As he parks in his office car park, he muses that when he was a child, his whole street seemed to know each other and that he used to love street footy. Now he knows the names of none of his neighbours, and can't think of the last time he spoke to them. As he enters the lift, his thoughts turn to his ever-increasing workload. He is worried with the turnover of staff in his area, about the increase in dissatisfied, and even angry, customers. He experiences inconsistent strategies and communications from his leaders. He knows what needs to happen to turn this decline around, yet he feels as if he has no ability to communicate this up to his leaders. He sees uncertainty and ambiguity everywhere he turns, feels despondent and stuck.

Sadly, this is all-too-common a picture. Anxiety, fear, anger, greed and lust seem to form the ever-growing fabric of a Red Zone world. Conversations in our workplace, like Gary's, tend to be dominated by transaction - what have you done, or not done as the case may be. If we were to ask Gary to describe his organisation's leadership, he may well observe:

An over-reliance on 'carrot and stick' strategies

The use of fear to drive performance

A perception, or indeed the reality of 'feathered nests' and other examples of self-serving power

An inability to integrate change and diversity while holding this as an expectation for those below

An inability to listen, understand and believe in their workforce

Leadership scholar, Jean Lipman-Blumen, defines toxic leaders as those whose "...destructive behaviours and dysfunctional personal characteristics generate serious and enduring poisonous effects...on those they lead". In our work we see plenty of toxic leadership, subtle and not-so-subtle. With an evolution towards distributed leadership in the form of senior leadership teams, we often see the impact of a single toxic leader on such teams. A single such leader of any team brings a significant cost to the group: leaders in the Red Zone deduct a great deal from their team, and their organisation.

There is an answer.

21st Century Leaders Need 21st Century Brains

Put very simply, leaders are people whom others want to follow. The desire to follow stems directly from the experience of being listened to, believed in and unconditionally respected. Through this, leaders create clarity of purpose, meaning of work and confidence to complete. Leaders help followers answer the questions:

Why are we all here?

What part do I play?

How can I be at my best?

To behave in a way that gives such answers to people, leaders need to have particular mind and brain states.

Given that emotions are contagious, and that the emotions of a leader are *most* contagious, being in the Blue Zone is very much a pre-requisite condition for providing listening, belief and respect to others.

Barry-Wehmiller is a not a household brand. Like us, you may well not have heard of this American packaging and automation giant. It turns over US$900 million a year, and has created 20% (compound) revenue and share value growth each year for the last nineteen years. Typically, stories of such growth are littered with razor gangs, outsourcing processes to cheap-labour countries and a ruthless approach to budgets and targets. Some years ago Robert Chapman, the CEO of Barry-Wehmiller, found his corporation facing soaring workers compensations costs. A common phenomenon for western corporations, his initial approach was conservative and expected: send out the message of the impact on the organisation of accidents and rising compensation costs. In other words, here was one measure of 'our company's' performance that is not up to par. Not surprisingly, the outcome was also conservative and expected: not much change.

In response, both to the situation and a desire to tie this situation more strongly to his personal leadership values, Chapman created a diverse team of 20 members from across the organisation to address workplace safety. This team posed a question: *"If we measure success by the way we touch the lives of people, then isn't safety really about the desire for each and every team member to arrive home safely each day?"* Through this question, and through the enabling leadership of Chapman, a 'key performance measure' move to being an integral value, through valuing people. At a keynote speech, Chapman said:

"Our problem in America is not our people. It's the lack of inspiration. It's the lack of people feeling fulfilled by what they're doing. We've gotten too disconnected from the way we touch the lives of people. Our promise at Barry-Wehmiller is that if we've got 4,100 employees and they each have an average of four people in their families, we've got more than 16,000 people directly impacted by our leadership. It is an awesome responsibility. How are you sending people home? Can they be there for their spouses, not just physically, but emotionally? For their kids? For their community? American business has a profound opportunity to have a sustained positive impact upon our society."

Norm Dean, now the Chief Education Consultant for the Middle East based company Educational Services Overseas Limited (ESOL), daily faces integrating the highly diverse skills, cultures and needs of both individual teachers and, indeed, whole schools. All of this in a culture that is not native to him. For him, it is critical that he operate from the Blue Zone, that he listens to observe, believes in those he leads and uses conversations for growth.

Illustrating this point was an occasion where one of the schools for which he has responsibility was undergoing a significant external review process. Just as this is a common issue for many school leadership teams, the feedback received from the process contained unexpected and challenging outcomes. Individual responses to the feedback ranged from internal to external blame, and typified the emotional Red Zone reaction that many of us express under these circumstances.

This is not an unusual situation for many leaders: the need to refocus the less-than-helpful energy of both individuals and the team towards finding a solution. Norm's approach was to work with individuals and the team by paying attention to:

Acknowledging the feedback as "This is how it is" (as observation) rather than interpretation (who is to blame?)

Unconditionally accepting and believing in the individuals on the team

Viewing the issue from the perspective of an impartial observer (from vision and planning, rather than from detail, problem or drama)

Directing the energy of the team towards tangibles (giving perceived autonomy) and the future solution (mobilising energy)

Through these attitudes and behaviours of Blue Zone leadership, he was able to help the individuals and the team grow to meet the challenge that this issue presented. As is very nearly always the case, the gain was not restricted to meeting the demands of this issue alone. Moreover, the team, through this form of leadership, has literally moved up a level in its capacity to meet other future challenges.

This form of leadership is not new to Norm. As a past Assistant Regional Director for the State Government Education Department in Victoria, and as a current high-level trainer of various Franklin Covey Leadership programs, he owes much of his success to his unconditional love and acceptance of all people, his capacity to separate the issue from the person and his ability to 'tell it as it is'. Indeed, the powerful mix of unconditional love for people with the ability to have the crucial conversations places him as one of the world's pre-eminent educational leaders.

> "...he owes much of his success to his unconditional love and acceptance of all people, his capacity to separate the issue from the person and his ability to 'tell it as it is'."

Chapman and Bowman are both 21st century leaders. Distilling most of what they do, say and believe into a common set of points, we see that they both:

- Believe in the people they lead
- Listen to the people they lead

- Unconditionally respect the people they lead
- Challenge both themselves and the people they lead towards personal and continual growth
- Have robust and significant skills of 'leadership delivery'

To authentically hold themselves to these values, attitudes and behaviours, they will undoubtedly have very high functioning in their Blue Zones. They will be very aware of their thinking and emotional states, will have many choices for these states, will be able to exercise these choices to a high degree, and will also be able to bring such awareness and choice to others.

They have 21st century brains.

The 'Three Brain' Evolution Of Our Education Systems

An observation that we would make is that our education systems, and indeed our western society, has evolved from a 'reptilian-brain' context to that of a 'mammalian-brain', parallel to the move from the industrial age to the information age. We are, right at this moment, experiencing the shift from mammalian-based (Red Zone) organizational structures to 'human-brain' Blue Zone organizations.

The reptilian brain is dominant when a baby is born and the human brain is not fully developed physically, until the child reaches their twenties.

The educative process is one of guiding the child so that the 'locus of control' that starts in the reptilian brain finally comes to rest in the human brain of the young adult. When this is the case we are at our best: bright, optimistic, collaborative and creative, and both the mammalian and reptilian brains fall into their appropriate supporting roles.

This runs smoothly if the baby receives appropriate social nurturance (loved and paid attention to) and cognitive stimulation (toys, stories, games, picture books, etc).

However, at the age of about ten the developing human brain becomes aware of its own existence and its own mortality – it is going to die – and presents this thought to the reptilian brain. This brain goes into fight/flight mode - but nothing works - and so goes into a state of anxiety, existential anxiety. Anxiety is biologically useless and if left unresolved will hinder further normal development and, as the child grows through the teenage years and into adulthood, will lead to increasingly desperate attempts to escape it. At the extreme this may lead to suicide, more generally to recurring bouts of depression, self-medication with alcohol or drugs, crime, inappropriate behaviours such as gangs and street violence, or promiscuity, devoid of affection, amongst other things.

Thus one of the most basic needs of an educative process is to help a child resolve this biologically useless and damaging anxiety.

State compulsory schooling was first set up by the Prussian State in a law enacted in 1819. The design for the mass of the population was to provide harsh discipline and rote learning that had the impact of providing for the child the belief that if they simply followed the rules they would be alright. This created a population that would rather kill or be killed on the battlefield than disobey an order, and that was accepting of boring and repetitive industrial jobs. However, people's existential anxiety was assuaged so that they acquiesced in this approach, and were happy, so to speak.

This system was copied and spread around the western, colonised and western-influenced world and was the regime in place until about the Second World War. One serious drawback of this approach is that adults are trapped into operating largely with the locus of control remaining in the reptilian brain, which limits cognitive development.

After the Second World War there began a process of reducing the harshness of the discipline, replacing rote learning with interesting and challenging content and increasing the time children spent at school. This all had the effect of shifting the locus of control from the reptilian brain to the mammalian brain, where we learn from experience and are grounded in reality, and gave readier access to the technical reason based in the human brain.

Under this regime, adults operating with the locus of control in the mammalian brain assuage their existential anxiety through conforming to a set of norms and being provided with security. Thus we saw the rise of cradle-to-grave social and health systems and jobs for life. The drawback of this approach is that adults are risk averse and generally uncreative, not too limiting in a relatively stable environment. Nevertheless, most people were content.

Towards the end of the 60's the social systems that supported this approach began to fray and respect for authority and authority figures began to decline. In the early 80's society prohibited corporal punishment in state schools and the conditions that traditionally assuaged existential anxiety (strict discipline, then conformance and security) became less effective.

Most successful adults can recall, on average, two teachers who had a substantial impact on their growth and development (this works out to be about 5% of teachers). Our own investigations, incorporating the latest neuroscience research, show that what these teachers are doing is causing the child's locus of control to shift into the human brain, to feel confident in themselves, confident in the future and have a sense of purpose – the keys to assuaging existential anxiety. So there is a third way to resolve the problem of existential anxiety, and that is to be in the presence of another human being (parent or teacher) who respects us, believes in us and listens to us (some of the key characteristics of outstanding teachers).

The bad news is that the proportion of teachers who do this is still about 5% (who are created despite the system, not because of it). The good news is that about 70-80% of children get this attention from their parents, which allows them to be OK (they would grow faster and further if they also got it for the 30 hours a week that they spend with teachers!). However, 20-30% do not get this attention from their parents and most of those do not get it from their teachers, either. This has had several implications over the last 30 years:

- 20-30% of children persistently lag behind in their ability to acquire a suitable education
- behaviour of many teens has deteriorated including an increase in teen suicides
- the status of teachers (and their relative earnings) has declined as they fail to meet their students' central need and society values what they are doing less

A central theme of our work is to create the conditions so that many more teachers can be like the 5% of outstanding teachers, and provide for children the conditions for them to shift into the 'human brain' state and become bright, optimistic, collaborative and creative.

Our action research has shown that the mind state of a teacher as they walk into a classroom is hugely determined by the culture of a school. If we want teachers to respect, believe in and listen to students, then they in turn need to be respected, believed in and listened to by others in the school. Shifting a culture or creating a new culture depends on leadership.

Importantly, the impact of an outstanding teacher as they walk into a classroom is entirely underpinned by the same Success Zone factors as the impact of an outstanding leader as they walk into a board room.

What works for Education works for the corporate world, as it does for the environment of the home.

Solving New Problems: The Real Need For Creativity

As we have seen from earlier in this book, the mammalian brain is where we store and retrieve learning from experience. This is hugely beneficial to us, and this functionality has historically served us well. However, this ability to solve known problems, even new variations of existing problems, through using prior experience, is beginning to fall short. Both the number and rate of new problems, that have no basis of prior experience, are placing huge demands on our decision-making and problem-solving architecture.

The new or 'human' brain, the seat of rational thinking, also has limits on its contribution. This cortical brain area, in spite of its massive rational capability, can only effectively process up to four variables. The limits of working memory for a single 'human' brain very much limit the complexity of a problem that can be considered and solved. In short, we have one brain - the mammalian brain - that can solve complex, but not new problems, and another - the human brain - that, on its own, can solve new, but not complex problems.

The answer? Harness more than one person's brain such that this group of brains operates in a creative, collaborative, generous and affiliative fashion. When these minds collaborate from a Blue Zone state, we have available the collective learning from experience and an ability to consider many more than four variables. We would call this a Blue Zone team, and it would be led by someone who, themselves, is strongly operating from their Blue Zone. Indeed, what makes this different from any previous description of an effective team is the strategic use of language, attitude and behaviour towards a collective Blue Zone experience.

For such a team to be truly solving contemporary issues, it will have to be well versed in Basic Conversations, it will need to have had all the necessary Crucial Conversations, and it will need to be facilitated in such a way that Generative Conversations can emerge.

This is already beginning to happen.

Distributed Leadership

Even as recently as five years ago, the all-powerful singular head of a school, the headmaster or principal, was not an uncommon form of school leadership. A quiet revolution has been taking place, not only in school leadership, but in broad organisational leadership also. This is the revolution of a collaboration of leadership brains towards solving new complex problems. We would see this shift as a 'Darwinian' response to the failure of singular brains in solving emerging issues never before experienced.

Yet while we now have a structure of leadership arising to meet contemporary challenges facing our world, the capacity of these teams often fall short. Creative future solutions to new problems can only emerge from a group when all of the members are in the Blue Zone. Any residual anxiety or fear will white-ant the generative process, often in ways undetectable to much, if not all, of the team.

Hence, individually and collectively, members of such 'generative' teams need the skills of self mastery (self awareness and self management), the behaviours of engagement (respect, listening to and believing in) and the ability to have any of the Four Conversations.

A Blueprint For Creating Blue Zone Organisations

So we have seen that we need leaders to have 21st Century Brains, brains that allow a mind state to be heavily biased toward the Blue Zone. We do, however, have a situation where the numbers of such people are relatively low. The good news is that the Blue Zone brain architecture can be reverse engineered. By learning to hold certain behaviours and attitudes, leaders, indeed anyone, can rewire themselves to have stronger Blue Zone function. Through the agency of neuroplasticity, the repetition of an action-reflection cycle that focuses on particular behaviours has already been proven to enable change. This change to a Blue Zone state has worked at both the individual and organisational level.

Case studies on such changes are available at http://www.thesuccesszone.com/resources.

In these case studies, we have seen significant shifts towards thriving cultures by creating the space for the following things to happen:

Creating a common language around the desired (and its opposite, undesired) mind state for learning (and therefore also change) to take place. Remember that people are bright, optimistic, collaborative and creative operating in their Blue Zones and self-centred, dull, pessimistic, moody and wary when operating in their Red Zones.

Giving senior leaders the experience and practice of bringing other people into the Blue Zone mind state, using basic conversations. This focuses on extending their questioning skills beyond questions that are useful to them (i.e. the leader) to ones that are useful to the other person. This extension also applies to a leader's ability to listen, extending their repertoire to listening styles that are useful to the other person. The effort required to do this helps a leader to reduce their own Red Zone activation and stay more often in the Blue Zone i.e. to be at their best.

Individually coaching each senior leader over three sessions to allow them to investigate and develop how they can be at their best (i.e. in the right mind state) more of the time.

Giving senior leaders the experience and practice of resolving issues when there is conflict or other difficulties present using crucial conversation, providing a process for them to visualise what their organisation could be like. Further we show them how their team would need to be to achieve this imagined future, begin the process of team members investigating what they bring to the team when at their best and what they subtract when in the wrong mind state, and what values they each hold and bring to the team.

Individually coaching each senior leader over a further three sessions to allow them to develop strength in holding crucial conversations and having open conversations within the team.

Giving senior leaders the experience and practice of having completely open, creative and transformative conversations - generative conversations - and drawing strategic decisions and operational plans from these conversations.

This process takes place over about 8-10 months (an academic year) and is a powerful means of developing individual leaders and leadership teams in an environment characterised by difference. As a process, it has evolved over time in response to what works, or what does not work, when trying to transform a school with over a hundred schools in Victoria and England. The process also extends to middle leaders and teachers themselves – obviously leaders in their own right. However, our work has shown that the greatest point of leverage in transforming a school lies with the senior leadership team and resolving the differences that lie within through a focus on changing how people behave with each other.

As organisations, schools are typically time poor and highly change resistant. The absence of a systemic mechanism (such as coaching) and the time to give any mechanism traction has led to entrenched leadership and instructional practices.

Schools are amongst the most difficult organisations to change. Yet we are seeing significant, and at times, rapid change when the enablers above are implemented. We continue to discover that the concepts covered in this book, and our programs, apply to an increasing breadth of contexts and situations.

So Where Are The Outstanding Leaders?

Our research, now conducted over the last eight years with over sixty thousand students, points to a relative paucity of outstanding teachers. On the cognisance of students, only about five percent of teachers are inspiring, creative, collaborative and highly engaging. To test this, try thinking, yourself, about how many outstanding teachers you can recall from your school years. We often ask this question, and we most often get the answer of between zero and three outstanding teachers. Most people will have had between thirty to fifty teachers in their school life - again roughly five percent. Less than a handful being outstanding. These outstanding teachers, themselves leaders in the classroom, are not the result of our teacher training and education systems - they are there in spite of these systems.

Similarly, our corporate, government and social organisations do have examples, like Robert Chapman, of outstanding Blue Zone leadership. Just as in teaching, these examples are isolated and very much tend not to be an outcome of our corporate, government or social organisation systems. In our own thinking and experience, we would struggle to find a more optimistic figure than five percent of the world's leadership being outstanding.

In other words, we have a huge shortfall in inspirational, collaborative, bright, creative, Blue Zone leaders. Everywhere.

Take a moment to consider the impact of changing this. Recall your best, most influential teacher. Recall, too, how many of your teachers were like this. Now imagine school as you remember it, with half of your teachers as if they were your best. What would it have been like? What would have been the impact of half your teachers, not one or two, believing in you, listening to you, stretching you?

How many people are like this in your workplace - people who believe in, listen and respect you? What would your workplace be like if you doubled this number? What would it be like if you were like this, yourself, for all who know you?

In his recent book, 'The Element', Sir Ken Robinson says: "Farmers base their livelihoods on raising crops. But farmers do not make plants grow. They don't attach the roots, glue on the petals or colour the fruit. The plant grows itself. Farmers and gardeners provide the conditions for growth. Good farmers know what those conditions are, and the bad ones don't. Understanding the dynamic elements of human growth is as essential to sustaining human cultures into the future as the need to understand the ecosystems of the natural work on which we ultimately depend."

Outstanding leaders know what the conditions for human growth are. Poor ones don't. You don't have to be responsible for hundreds of employees and a big budget to qualify for leadership. Where there is a need for you to create the conditions for someone else to grow, then you fit the remit of a leader.

As a parent, friend, teacher or manager, all can be and should be leaders from the Blue Zone.

Glossary of Terms

Blue Zone:
The mind state that is expressed through a dominance of brain activity in the 'human' and 'mammalian' brains.

Red Zone:
The mind state that is expressed through a dominance of brain activity in the 'reptilian' and 'mammalian' brains.

Amygdalae (plural), Amydala (singular):
Almond-shaped 'bodies' located deep within the medial temporal lobes of the brain in complex vertebrates, including humans. Shown in research to perform a primary role in the processing and memory of emotional reactions, the amygdalae are considered part of the limbic system. Amongst many other functions, the amygdalae are responsible for the genesis of many fear responses, including freezing (immobility), tachycardia (rapid heartbeat), increased respiration, and stress-hormone release.

Tripartite Brain
Also called the triune brain, the tripartite brain is a model proposed by Paul D. MacLean where, the brain is broken down into three separate brains that have their own special intelligence, subjectivity, sense of time and space, and memory. The triune brain consists of the reptilian, mammalian and the human brain.

Mammalian Brain

Also known as the mid or limbic brain, this region is the emotional seat of our brain. It is also where we learn from experience.

In the Success Zone model, the mammalian brain is common to both the Blue and Red Zones.

Human Brain

Also known as the neocortex, or the cortical brain, this region is the youngest (in evolutionary terms) part of the brain, and the last to mature. It is responsible for (amongst a myriad of things) rational thought, language, social interconnectivity, setting goals, monitoring errors and self-identity.

In the Success Zone model, it combines with the mammalian brain to create the Blue Zone.

Reptilian Brain

The reptilian brain is the oldest (in evolutionary terms) region of the brain. While it is so named for the presence of similar brain function and form as found in reptiles, in reality is more developed in humans than it is in reptiles. It seems to control normal involuntary behavior that the conscious mind does not, such as the cardiac and respiratory functions

Glossary of Terms

It is also responsible for rage and basic survival fight-or-flight responses. In humans, it is a region of the brain that plays an important role in the integration of sensory perception, coordination and motor control.

A significant element of the reptilian brain is the cerebellum, and modern research shows that the cerebellum has a broader role in a number of key cognitive functions, including attention and the processing of language, music, and other sensory temporal stimuli. The cerebellum is also the centre of habit: motor and cognitive habits have their 'circuitry' here.

Coaching

Coaching is a discipline where a range of attitudinal, behaviour and language skills merge, towards helping another think better about a situation, problem or dilemma. The act of coaching is often more beneficial for the coach, given the need to listen strongly to the coachee for the coachee, thus exercising development in self awareness and self management.

Prefrontal Cortex

The prefrontal cortex is a special region of the 'human' or cortical brain. Sometimes called the executive brain, this region is thought to act like the conductor of an orchestra, coordinating the activity of many other brain regions.

This brain region has been implicated in planning complex cognitive behaviors, personality expression, decision making and moderating correct social behavior, recognizing faces and emotions and inferring the internal emotional states of others. The basic activity of this brain region is considered to be orchestration of thoughts and actions in accordance with internal goals.

References, Resources And Further Reading

The references below are a range of resources and further reading from authors and organisations that have influenced our work, or that add to the story of this book in some way.

An up to date page with links to videos mentioned is available on http://www.thesuccesszone.com/resources.

Matt Church
http://www.mattchurch.com.au/
Matt Church is without a shadow of a doubt one of our country's most established, enduring and successful professional speakers. It is however his phenomenal ability to teach that sets him apart from any other communication educator.
He is the creator of the global Thought Leaders movement and is the coach behind some of the greatest speakers this country has produced.

Juan Aguilera
http://www.thecrucialquarter.com/
Juan is currently Managing Director of 'The Crucial Quarter' and has extensive experience working with individuals and organisations to create changes, increase performance and achieve goals. His clients range from large organisations

such as Lion Nathan, AMP and NAB through to not for profit organisations working in the area of social justice. He particularly works with leaders in the crucial first 90 days of their leadership.

Dr Matthew Liberman & Dr Naomi Eisenberger
The pains and pleasures of social life: a social cognitive neuroscience approach
Neuroleadership Journal Issue One 2008

Thomas Lewis, Fari Amini and Richard Lannon
A General Theory of Love (IBSN 0375709223)

David Rock
Quiet Leadership (IBSN 9780060835910)

Barry Schwartz
Psychology of Learning and Behaviour (IBSN 978-0393975918)

Video on the loss of wisdom (TED Conference 2009):
http://www.ted.com/talks/barry_schwartz_on_our_loss_of_wisdom.html)

Jonah Lehrer
The Decisive Moment (IBSN 9781921520105)

References, Resources And Further Reading

Dr Kevin Ochsner
Staying cool under pressure: insights from social cognitive neuroscience
Neuroleadership Journal Issue One 2008

Susan Scott
Fierce Conversations: Achieving Success at Work (IBSN 0425193373)

Barry-Wehmiller
Inspirational Leadership - The Barry Wehmuller Story:
http://www.bizmanualz.com/information/2007/06/18/inspirational-leadership-the-barry-wehmiller-story.html

Sir Ken Robinson
http://www.sirkenrobinson.com
The Element (IBSN 9781846142659)

Video on how schools kill creativity (TED Conference 2006):
http://www.ted.com/talks/lang/eng/ken_robinson_says_schools_kill_creativity.html

Mick Cope
The Seven Cs of Coaching (IBSN 978 0 273 68110 6)

Organisations:

emergent•blue: http://www.emergentblue.com

Group 8 Education: http://www.gr8education.com

Group 8 Management: http://www.gr8management.com

emergent•blue is a new entity formed by *Group 8 Management* that is specifically seeking to foster Blue Zone leadership and capacity in our world.

emergent•blue provide professional development that incorporates recent research into how our brains handle change and that fosters the best conditions for stimulating learning and change in both adults and children. The authors of this book are the three principal partners of *emergent•blue*. Grown out of the action research heritage undertaken by Group 8 Education in the Education space, *emergent•blue* is now applying its intellectual property in the Not-For-Profit, Corporate and Government contexts.

Thought Leaders Global: http://www.thoughtleaders.com.au/
Thought Leaders Global assists clever people to be commercially smart using a revolutionary business model. A framework for doing business better, faster and easier that's poised to change the way business is conducted forever. More of a movement than an organisation, Thought Leaders helps their members achieve financial freedom faster!

Organisations

TED
http://www.ted.com/

TED is a small nonprofit devoted to Ideas Worth Spreading. It started out (in 1984) as a conference bringing together people from three worlds: Technology, Entertainment, Design. A free and leading source of inspiration and innovation, this resource is a must for any thought leader.

Star Wards/Bright
http://www.starwards.org.uk

Star Wards is a project run by the UK charity Bright that suggests, collects and publicises ideas that enable mental health inpatients to make the best use of their time in hospitals.

International Coach Federation:
http://www.coachfederation.org/

The International Coach Federation is the largest worldwide resource for professional coaches, and the source for those who are seeking a coach. They are a nonprofit organization formed by individual members-professionals who practice coaching, including Executive Coaches, Leadership Coaches, Life Coaches and many more, from around the world.

Australian and New Zealand Institute of Coaching
www.anzicoaching.com

Peak professional association, providing support, supervision and professional development for Coaches.

Author Backgrounds

Andrew Mowat

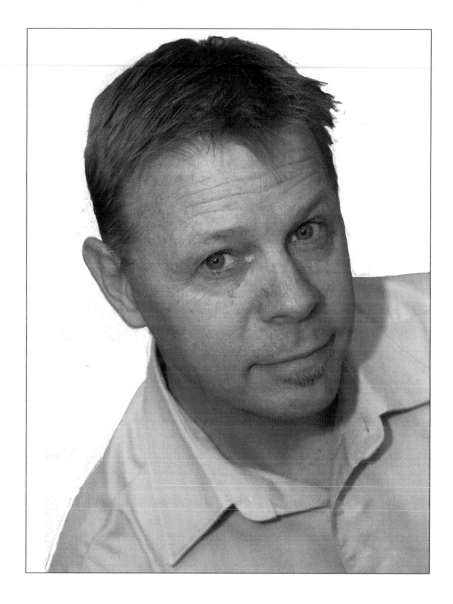

Author Backgrounds

Qualifications
B.Sci.Ed (Melbourne)
Accredited Results Coaching Systems Coach (Executive Coaching)
New York University Certification ~ Precursors to Coaching

The Vision
Through committed and accountable coaching, my clients strive towards inspiring goals and enjoy a stretching journey of learning, creating capacity and realizing resilient success.

My training immerses participants in the methodology, giving real and experiential learning to the challenge of stepping away from our default and inefficient communications styles.

Audiences enjoy and gain much from my speaking engagements, where I connect through the story emerging from leadership, neuroscience and coaching. Humour, translating the science and connecting the message to people's own experience are hallmarks of my style.

The Story
Professionally, I have accrued over 22 years working with people of all ages in the education sector, with many and varied contexts (mainstream, primary, secondary, TAFE, Koorie) and roles (student welfare, technology leadership, school leadership). The last 6 years of my time in education

were spent as a school principal. Here, strong emotional intelligence and people skills were expressed towards providing inspirational leadership in a complex setting. Through this, I created a learning and improvement culture and facilitated individual potential and organizational capacity.

My move into coaching in 2004 allowed me to focus my capacity to engage others in their own growth. Since then, I have built a strong 'portfolio' of executive and leadership coaching and coach training. Indeed, training others to coach has deepened my own understanding and skill in coaching itself. I now coach, particularly in the field of organizational leadership, and train coaches throughout Australia and the United Kingdom

I am now a Principal Partner in Group 8 Education. Here, we focus on helping transform organizational cultures into places where all thrive. Based on brain-based coaching, we teach leaders how to engage themselves and others in growth and adaptation.

Through this journey as a professional coach, trainer, public speaker and author my passion for people and their potential has deeper clarity and purpose. My background, training and experience all serve to allow a strong and committed connection with organizations and individuals. Via this connection, and with the use of strong coaching systems and tools, coachees and participants experience focus, reflection, humour, growth and learning.

Author Backgrounds

John Corrigan

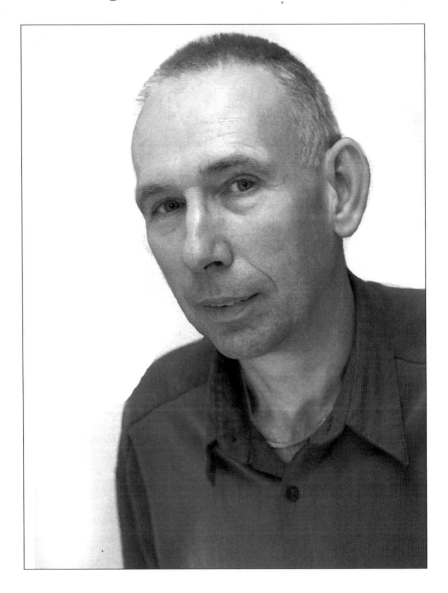

Qualifications:
MA (cantab), MBA

The Vision

I had become good at understanding how businesses worked and how you changed them to get better performance. One of the key lessons was that if you want to get different outcomes then you must hold different assumptions. About twelve years ago I decided to apply this lesson to myself. To my shock I discovered that nothing I held to be true or sacred stood up to scrutiny. Nothing.

After all the fall out, what was left to me to hold onto were three things:

- I don't want anyone to tell me what to do, and I don't want to tell anyone what they should do, either (so if I want to create something that needs other people then I need to do so in a way that gets their willing involvement)

- we are all connected and if I do something good for you it is also good for me – so why would I ever do anything bad to anyone?

- life has direction and that direction is towards greater richness and complexity and what supports that is good, so that is what I should do.

Author Backgrounds

After a while I decided that I must live with these principles as the basis of my life. What an amazing journey that has been.

The Story

A varied career spanning nine countries and almost as many industries gradually led to a desire to do "something with meaning" rather than simply having a senior role in a corporation.

Becoming CEO of an environmental technology start-up was a first step out and a tremendous learning experience in moving away from the safety of a large organisation. Gradually, it became clear, however, that you get a bigger bang for your buck in social change rather than technological change prompting the search for a role somewhere in that area. Two years later, the opportunity to spend a day looking at the education sector triggered the sudden realisation that that is where I wanted to be. I set myself ten years to see the transformation of our education systems and started working in my spare time with a local school to understand the issues and, very importantly, identify the systemic problems that were causing the sector to fail to meet society's needs.

After 18 months a move to working full time led to setting up Group 8 Education as a trading entity of Group 8

Management and switching focus to Victoria – very open to innovation in education. The next five years provided an increasing depth of understanding of the problems that face the education sector and the gradual emergence of ways to solve them. Most recently it has become clear that education represents a special case in a more general shift that is taking place across organisations world-wide.

Previously Published:

A World fit for Children

Author Backgrounds

Douglas Long

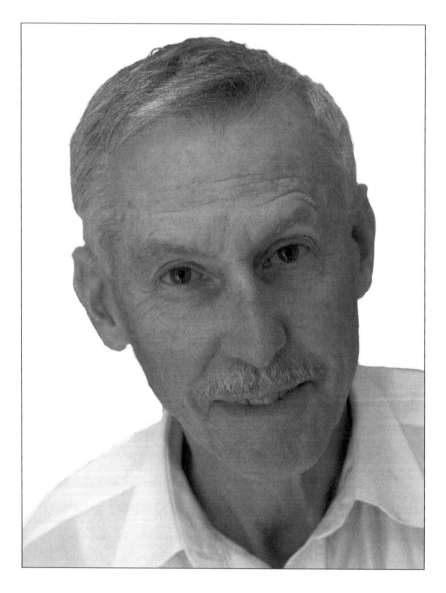

Qualifications:
BA, LTh, PhD

The Vision

To the west of Sydney in the state of New South Wales, Australia, are the "Blue Mountains." To my mind they are one of the most beautiful places in the world. Often I have stood at one of the lookouts and seen in the distance a rainbow cutting its way through the mist and blending into the bush some kilometres away. Between where I have stood and the end of the rainbow has been a vast chasm or canyon – hundreds of metres deep and with steep, bush clad walls.

Some years ago I was up there with some friends who were visiting from the USA. The day was fine but thunder clouds were rolling in. In the distance the rain storm could be seen galloping across the valley. A particularly beautiful rainbow was shimmering against a rapidly darkening, very sombre background. Close to me and my friends stood a father and his young son admiring the same view. "Daddy," said the boy, "take me to the rainbow."

We all need rainbows in our lives. They are the ideal that we can imagine. But rainbows are ephemeral. If we want to reach their end – the place with the pot of gold – we need something more solid: a compass bearing or GPS-identified location. That is the role of a vision.

For over 30 years the idealist in me has seen the rainbow – a world in which conditions continually improve for every person regardless of age, sex, race, nationality, sexual orientation, language, colour or any other discriminator. My practical side has focused on a series of visions – time specific sharply focused pictures of what can realistically be achieved. Now in my mid 60's the time available to me to help facilitate change is obviously shorter than it has been – but the vision, and rainbow, remain.

The Story

Having obtained my PhD as a mature age student – I was in my 40's – and with a keen interest in leadership, I was fortunate to be able to spend the 12 years to 2000 researching, developing and teaching the program "Leadership in Senior Management" at Macquarie Graduate School of Management in Sydney. At the same time I was consulting to a broad range of organisations in the public, private, and not-for-profit sectors in the areas of leadership and change. This work took me throughout South East Asia and I was invited as a keynote speaker to conferences throughout the world. Through these activities I was able to see change and growth in both organisations and people.

But something was missing.

In 2001 a colleague and I formed Group 8 Management and a few years later we were fortunate to be joined by John Corrigan who had committed himself to understanding why the earnings and status of teachers had suffered serious decline over recent decades. We formed Group 8 Education to study and remedy this problem. A further few years and we were joined by Andrew Mowat who added the coaching component that was so necessary.

The work done primarily by John and Andrew has supplied the piece that we always knew was missing – but couldn't find. This is the understanding that, underlying all successful change we find a shift in the brain circuitry from a rapid, stimulus response, fight, flight or freeze mechanism; through a circuitry in which affiliation and feeling dominates; to a new world – the "Blue Zone" – in which that part of the brain which makes us truly human is able to come into its own.

Now I work with organisations and people - bringing my dream to fulfilment and on making my vision a reality – in the knowledge that with this new learning the requisite change can be long term and extremely positive in every arena of life.

It is also of great value in my work as a DBA Supervisor with Southern Cross University Graduate College of Management where I work with mature age students seeking to obtain their Doctor in Business Administration.

Previously Published:

Learner Managed Learning: the key to life long learning and development

Competitive Advantage in the 21st Century: from vision into action

The Challenge of the Diamond

Leaders: diamonds or cubic zirconia